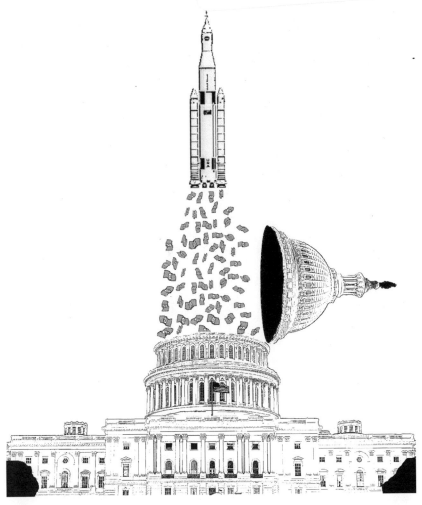

The Plundering of NASA: an Exposé

(How pork barrel politics harm American spaceflight leadership)

R.D. Boozer, MoA (in astrophysics)

ISBN 978-1-300-93906-1

Lulu.com

To my wife and love of my life, Julie

The wind beneath my wings.

Also, with reverence and admiration, to all of the American scientists, engineers, technicians and astronauts whose efforts over the last half century made our country a leader in the Final Frontier.

May your great legacy be adapted to fit the realities of a new era.

Contents

Prologue... 1

Chapter 1: Learning the wrong lesson 11

Chapter 2: Common detrimental myths about spaceflight................. 15

2.1 Myth: For ambitious exploration, NASA needs a large budget increase. 15

2.2 Myth: NASA designed and developed rockets are safer........... 16

2.3 Myth: Shuttle-derived vehicles are safer. 16

2.4 Myth: Shuttle-derived vehicles are developed faster and cheaper. 17

2.5 Myth: Safety cannot be regulated too much. 19

2.6 Myth: Build SLS or the Chinese will own space! 24

2.7 Myth: Chemical powered rockets have to be expensive to fly. 24

2.8 Myth: The Commercial Crew Program hinders space exploration. 25

2.9 Myth: Depots are useless unless they are restocked from the Moon.. 26

2.10 Myth: Space stations and depots require heavy lift rockets. ... 27

2.11 Myth: Human space flight must hurt robotic space exploration. 27

2.12 Myth: Reusable rockets don't save money............................. 28

2.13 Myth: Russians are hauling Americans to ISS because of Obama.. 28

2.14 Myth: The G.W. Bush administration messed up the Shuttle. 29

2.15 Myth: Relying on Russia never happened before................... 30

2.16 Myth: All NASA launchers and spacecraft are "commercial" vehicles. 30

Chapter 3: The paradox of SLS 33

3.1 The genesis of SLS 34

3.2 The gorging on SLS pork begins 35

3.3 The call for more practical alternatives to SLS 39

3.4 The hypocrisy of some SLS supporters 42

3.5 Robbing Peter to pay Paul 44

3.6 Evidence that SLS is not practical 45

Chapter 4: Why is SLS outrageously expensive compared to alternatives? 47

4.1 Cost-plus contracting and FAR 48

4.2 The "Whittle-knife Effect" 50

4.3 Negative effects of a finished and functioning SLS 57

Chapter 5: A practical, affordable and *ambitious* national space program *starting now* 63

5.1 A truly innovative proposal from ULA 63

5.2 The suppression of NASA's ground-breaking propellant depot report 65

5.3 The initial Georgia Tech and NASA reports 66

5.4 Evidence of incorrect assumptions by ASAP 68

5.5 The need for in-space infrastructure 71

5.6 Attempted hijacking of the in-space infrastructure issue 74

5.7 Other needed technologies that SLS inhibits 78

5.8 Building the first true spaceship 80

5.9 "Farmers", "the Committee" and "Tinkerbells" 83

5.10 Determining who will *honestly* consider the evidence against SLS 84

5.11 What is really important to insure American space supremacy? 87

Chapter 6: The transition to the Commercial Cargo and Commercial Crew Programs 89

6.1 A power grab to protect the pork 90

6.2 The Congressional propaganda smokescreen 93

6.3 Advantages of multiple Commercial Crew participants 94

6.4 The Commercial Crew down-selection effort 96

6.5 SLS, Commercial Crew and the sequester 97

6.6 SLS and the Chinese 97

6.7 Congressional SLS supporters unknowingly harm their constituents 101

6.8 ASAP recommendations that could harm American space leadership 104

Chapter 7: NASA as technology incubator *and* cutting edge space explorer 113

7.1 The ultimate source of American space technology 113

7.2 NASA as explorer and frontier expander 117

Chapter 8: The way to American supremacy in space 119

8.1 The space industry culture of risk aversion 119

8.2 A difference in attitude: new space companies versus old 122

8.3 Lack of innovation is not just a U.S. problem 127

8.4 The "can-do" attitude of SpaceX 128

8.5 American moxie is not confined to SpaceX 130

Chapter 9: It's up to *us*! 131

H.R.1702: The Commercial Space Act of 1998 137

Glossary of Space Related Terms 165

References 179

Acknowledgements 191

Table of Illustrations

Figure 1: All of the original Commercial Crew Program participants (Image credit: NASA) 5

Figure 2: Saturn V Moon Rocket (Image Credit: NASA)..................11

Figure 3: Falcon 9 launching cargo in Dragon spacecraft (Image credit: NASA)..18

Figure 4: Early Atlas rocket with Mercury spacecraft (Image credit: NASA)..20

Figure 5: Titan rocket launching Gemini spacecraft (Image credit: NASA)..21

Figure 6: The modern Atlas V and Delta IV launcher families (Image Credit: AFSPC/PA)..22

Figure 7: Proposed propellant depot (Image credit: NASA).................25

Figure 8: Russian Soyuz spacecraft bringing passengers to ISS (Image credit: NASA) 29

Figure 9: A Space Shuttle launch (Image credit: NASA)..................30

Figure 10: Proposed smaller and larger versions of SLS (Image credit: NASA)..34

Figure 11: Proposed VASIMR engine on ISS (Image credit: NASA).......43

Figure 12: Ares-1X on the launch pad (Image credit: NASA)..............51

Figure 13: An expanded view of SLS Block 1 (Image credit: NASA)......54

Figure 14: An expanded view of SLS Block 2 (Image credit: NASA)......55

Figure 15: Artist's conception of Falcon Heavy (Image credit: SpaceX) 61

Figure 16: A proposed inflatable gateway (Image credit: NASA) 73

Figure 17: Cut-away showing interior of the Bigelow BEAM (Image credit: NASA) 77

Figure 18: NAUTILUS-X (Image credit: NASA)...................................81

Figure 19: Orion-MPCV (Image credit: NASA) 114

Figure 20: Dragon spacecraft (Image credit: SpaceX) 115

Figure 21: Dream Chaser space plane (Image credit: Sierra Nevada) 117

Figure 22: Light areas indicate possible water ice at Mercury's poles seen from Messenger spacecraft (Image credit: NASA).....................118

Figure 23: Grasshopper reusable test vehicle in flight (Image credit: SpaceX)... 122

Figure 24: Scale model prototype test for Reusable Booster System project (Image credit: AFRL) 124

Figure 25: Diagram of Orion flight abort with LES (Image credit: NASA) 127

Prologue

"We have met the enemy, and he is us!"
-- from the comic strip **Pogo**[1]

From the late nineteen sixties to the early seventies, American astronauts went to the Moon, not once, but several times. In the decades since, we have been stuck doing only trips to low Earth orbit without the epic exploration voyages that were anticipated for the beginning of the twenty-first century in the movie *2001: A Space Odyssey*. There have been many articles and books written as to why this magnificent future did not come to pass. Even though most of these writings came to conclusions that were based on seemingly reasonable evidence, it is now apparent to a number of people that much of the accepted wisdom as to what went awry is ***grossly*** incorrect. This criticism even applies to some fairly recent writings and testimonies on the subject by a few of my fellow scientists and aerospace engineers. What's more, some former astronauts, for whom I have the greatest respect and who happen to be lifelong heroes of mine, seem to dogmatically accept a number of these misconceptions as truths that are virtually set in stone.

In this book, I will be putting forth solutions that are *other people's* ideas rather than my own. **Primarily, I will be presenting the results of scientific studies conducted by or at the behest of <u>NASA itself</u>, the aerospace industry and major universities**. Studies done by renowned and knowledgeable professionals, whose work extends deeply into the fields to be discussed and for which there is *substantial* supporting evidence as to their scientific and technical validity. My own scientific knowledge as a cutting-edge astrophysics researcher and my extensive technical background is merely a means by which I am able to judge which ideas are valid and which are not. My years of experience as a tutor to struggling high school and college physics students will also help me explain to the reader the "whys" and the "wherefores" of the subject matter in fairly

---

[1] Kelly, Walt; 1953; *Pogo Papers, The;* Simon & Schuster, New York, "Forward"

common less technical language. In other words, I will be the reader's translator of advanced scientific and engineering jargon into more understandable everyday English.

As a prelude to my full explanation of both the problems and solutions to NASA's current predicament, the reader should know how I came to write this book.

I have been an enthusiast of all things related to outer space as long as I can remember, including human spaceflight. Every clear night that was available to me as a boy was spent under the stars with my telescope. During my youth I designed and built many a rocket and even made my own rocket engines (much to the chagrin of my mother and the utter bafflement of my father). There is a part of me that is the logical calculating scientist: the astrophysics researcher who applies mathematics and physics on a daily basis to my advanced scientific work. On the other hand, there is a more emotional side of me that is enticed by the excitement and romance of space travel. Instead of just remotely exploring the universe from a distance with a telescope, I'd actually like to travel there.

It is the purpose of this book, not only to bring to light what is hurting America's advancement into the space frontier, but also to highlight those **positive aspects** *that are propelling us forward toward a time when I and other citizens of modest means can take a flight to orbit or beyond. And yes, I also wish to recommend specific steps forward based on the work of some brilliant and talented aerospace professionals: steps that can maintain the United States* **as the leading spacefaring nation of the twenty-first century**, *because I am first and foremost a proud American.*

Now, touching on the political aspects of what will be discussed …

Some of the very politicians who claim to be supporters of both a strong NASA and a robust American human spaceflight capability have been instigators of its decline. Many, perhaps *most*, are good Americans causing harm unwittingly due to ignorance or bad advice. In a few instances, the harm may have been done in an outrageous or even egregious manner even when the overall intent was beneficent. In these cases, certain public officials of **both** main political parties have brought about a gradual eroding of our national competitiveness in both exploring and economically **exploiting** the last great physical frontier above our heads. Some even do this while erroneously proclaiming the Chinese will come to dominate space if we don't follow their advice. But in reality, their actions are to the detriment of the very national competiveness they profess to be protecting and in so doing allow the Chinese to gradually wear away our now considerable technical lead. Indeed, through their ignorance they are harming NASA's efforts that would benefit and enhance the standard of living and quality of life of our citizenry; evidence of which will be revealed in the following pages.

Many who claim to be supporters of NASA hurt it by grabbing dollars from its budget for pork barrel projects that they **claim** (and possibly may even **believe**) are legitimate spaceflight endeavors done for the good of the entire country, but that in reality only provide **temporary economic benefits** to small specific areas of the country or certain corporate interests whilst sacrificing our **national** competiveness in the high frontier.

There also exist a couple of groups which are true foes of NASA. The first are those people who completely denigrate human spaceflight and question its value to the Republic. These are the people who would have the dollars allocated for human spaceflight in NASA's budget go to other possible uses, even though NASA's *total* budget for human spaceflight, robotic spaceflight and aeronautics is a drop in the proverbial bucket compared to most other programs and agencies: about 0.003 - a mere three one-thousandths - of the overall federal budget.

The other group, believe it or not, are spaceflight advocates who think NASA should be eliminated because *some* fairly influential mid- and upper-level officials within the agency either actively oppose or inadvertently inhibit the lowering of spaceflight costs that can be accomplished through using launch vehicles and spacecraft whose design and development are not minutely managed by NASA. The reasons for this group's attitude are not totally groundless, as I will show. However, this group's position does not take into account the economic advantages to the commercial space industry of a government agency that develops cutting-edge technology while conducting risky exploratory missions that are too expensive for the private commercial space sector to develop entirely on its own. They don't see the value in having NASA technologically accelerate the commercial space industry forward in the manner that its predecessor NACA did for commercial aviation. That earlier agency's decades of financing and conducting unprofitable aviation research was a major factor allowing airline travel to become safer and more economical by leaps and bounds within a historically short period of time. Neither do they see the advantage of NASA acting as a customer for space launch vehicles and spacecraft supplied by the still developing commercial spaceflight industry, filling the equivalent vital role as the U.S Postal Service in kick-starting commercial aviation in its early years when airline passenger service was still struggling to be profitable.

*With evidence supplied by world class scientists, engineers and space policy experts (including the faction of prominent former and current astronauts and NASA executives who have made a concerted effort towards keeping their knowledge current over the last few decades), I will prove herein, that the actions of the political pork barrel group have been far more effective at hurting NASA and American space prowess than **anything** attempted by both self-proclaimed anti-spaceflight people and anti-NASA people of the* *other variety*. These actions are the "Plundering of NASA" that is alluded to in the title of this book.

Within these pages you will find example after example of such detrimental actions. But if I as author only related those incidents, then these chapters would be merely a useless exercise in chest pounding brought on by frustration or despair. Instead, *my only reason for relating these facts is to give the reader the depth of understanding that he or she needs to comprehend the steps that are necessary for fixing the problems.*

I consider myself to be one of NASA's greatest fans. To stand idly by and see this organization of extraordinarily talented people mistakenly *forced* along an inappropriate path and getting the blame for the ensuing negative results is something I and others find intolerable. Hence, the creation of this written work, which *I hope* you will take the time to read and ponder deeply; not just for my sake, but for yours and for the sake of generations of Americans who will follow us.

As a youth, I was inspired by the science fiction books of Heinlein, Clark, Asimov, Bradbury, et cetera. Heinlein's vision was primarily one where the forces of free enterprise are unleashed to conquer space, as he described in the 1950s sci-fi movie "Destination Moon" and his classic science fiction novel "The Man Who Sold the Moon". And that relates to why progress in spaceflight in the real world has been slow in comparison to the earlier development of aviation. Part of the problem for several decades has been the lack of free enterprise competition in the space arena. Historically intense competition between companies has greatly lowered the cost of other forms of transportation and we are now finally starting to see such competition in the space arena. For a period of four decades we saw no decrease in human spaceflight costs because the only competition had been between national governments whose primary motivation was to get a strategic political or military advantage over their rival nation states. In this environment, lowering of costs was a secondary consideration when it was considered at all.

While reading this book you will see that there are some very good reasons to believe a significant drop in the cost of access to space -- similar to what was seen in other transportation industries -- will occur when commercial economic forces are finally **allowed** to **fully** work on spaceflight. The first government attempt to get the commercial space industry rolling was through the *Commercial Cargo* program to allow low cost transportation of supplies to the International Space Station. The second attempt (in the form of the *Commercial Crew Program*) is meant to end our reliance on the Russians for transport of American astronauts to ISS by sending them up on: 1) rockets from the commercial market which for *many years* have reliably launched civilian communications satellites and military satellites and 2) on some *new* commercially developed rockets *after* the new manufacturers had *proven* their vehicles' reliability with *a multitude* of safely executed launches. Indeed, the U.S. boasts a world-class stable of orbital launch vehicles provided by *Orbital Sciences, United Launch Alliance (ULA)*, and *Space Exploration Technologies (SpaceX)* that are second-to-none.

Besides highly capable launch vehicle manufacturers, a number of spacecraft manufacturers were initially chosen under NASA's Commercial Crew program to build orbital spacecraft to transport crew to the ISS with the idea that competition among them would ultimately lower prices. Those companies were: industry veteran *Boeing, SpaceX* (supplying *both* a spacecraft as well as a launch vehicle), *Sierra Nevada Corporation (SNC), Blue Origin, Alliant Tech Systems (ATK)* and *Excalibur ALMAZ*. It also should be noted that ULA was assigned to supply the launch vehicles for the SNC and Blue Origin spacecraft. However, it appears as though the purveyors of pork may have succeeded in substantially cutting much of the funding that is meant to promote this competition, though not completely. Indeed, concrete evidence will also be put forward on later pages supporting the contention that threatened special interests are behind the recent political efforts to winnow Commercial Crew participants as much as possible.

Figure 1: All of the original Commercial Crew Program participants (Image credit: NASA)

For years some of the politicians opposed to the Commercial Crew program conducted a propaganda campaign that publicly portrayed SpaceX as the only participant in the Commercial Crew program and to portray the proponents of this program as wanting to kill NASA and hand the whole human spaceflight budget over to SpaceX. This false impression was easy to spread simply because SpaceX had been in the news with its progress in the *Commercial Cargo program* that exists to send supplies to the International Space Station, while the other Commercial Cargo participant, *Orbital Sciences*, had yet to get much notice simply because it was off to a later start in the development of its launch vehicle and cargo spacecraft than SpaceX.

The reality is that all along, both the Commercial Cargo and Commercial Crew programs were intended to have multiple participants. Indeed, part of the very argument in favor of those programs was *always* that multiple participants are an advantage, for reasons that I will explain in coming pages. Ironically, the very politicians who complained about a nonexistent push for a SpaceX monopoly have been some of the principle advocates for cutting the program down to one Commercial Crew launch provider, which at this stage would have to be SpaceX simply because they've got a head start and are closer to being finished. These particular politicians in effect would be creating the very condition they have claimed to be so concerned about! But the real idea behind their efforts is to cut funds from Commercial Crew and reroute those monies to a particular Congressional earmark pork barrel space project whose specifics will be exposed shortly.

There is a delusionary position of many who support the status quo type of operation that NASA has been following for the last four decades. They claim, *despite* nonpartisan government and industry studies to the contrary, that had the Constellation project (the now cancelled purported effort to return Americans to the Moon) not been cancelled, the defunct Ares-1 launch vehicle would be working by now and the development of the Ares-V super launch vehicle would also be well under way. Again, the *overwhelming* evidence supporting the counter-position to this argument will be covered here in due course.

Costs of space access have already fallen substantially lately due to one company's aggressive emphasis on efficiency, but they need to descend even more. And no, this drop in launch price need not be at a loss of safety. *Indeed, I will present arguments to the reader that the trend toward commercial competition will have a **positive** effect on the safety of spaceflight.*

Our current suboptimal situation is further exacerbated by the fact that there is an ideological *schism* within the body of NASA's current and former (but still politically influential) upper/middle management. One faction only feels comfortable with the development of launchers derived from Space Shuttle technology using traditional NASA micro-supervised methods regardless of how much it costs both in money and manpower, whilst the other faction wants to hand over the essentially mundane tried and true process of launcher development to industry. The idea of the latter position being that it will significantly lower the cost of access to space; thereby, allowing the nation to get much more spacefaring done within budget and also *free NASA personnel to work on more technologically challenging* **highly** *advanced projects that are truly worthy of the agency's largely untapped potential.* The earlier mentioned pork motivated politicians naturally gravitate to members of the former NASA faction (sometimes referred to as the "Old Guard") to justify their actions, since the development of Shuttle-derived vehicles would employ the maximum number of their constituents who formerly worked on the Shuttle. Later pages of this book will provide hard evidence of this contention.

There is nothing wrong with politicians wanting to keep the maximum number of their constituents employed; in fact, as a general rule that is a good thing. But it can stifle the advancement of the Nation *as a whole* when politicians insist on the continuation of obsolete methods and technologies that no longer offer a competitive advantage. **What is supposed to be a Space Program should not be treated as though it is primarily a jobs program.** That attitude of deemphasizing groundbreaking space research and technology in favor of outmoded make-work (that gets us no real progress in space) is a dead-end that will eventually lead to an economy where workers will have an even harder time finding jobs that offer them a decent standard of living because they lack a modern skillset. In the long run, it is much more of an advantage for those same workers to be retrained in the state-of-the-art knowledge and skills that will keep America competitive far into the future and; in turn, insure that our international competitors do not leave us in the dust.

A new type of partnership of NASA with industry is what is needed and we are seeing the beginnings of such a partnership now. In this scenario NASA is the **technology incubator** for the commercial space industry as well as being a **customer** of that industry. Just as important, it also would be the **cutting-edge** *explorer* which conducts **both** manned and robotic deep space missions to the Moon and beyond. Those missions are projects that *initially* are not profitable, but that will later become commercially viable after NASA passes its internally developed spinoff tech to industry for refinement into profitability. Remember it was government sponsored exploratory expeditions by such notables as Lewis and Clark, Zebulon Pike, etc. that set the stage for the westward migration of people and industry that followed them into the American frontier. NASA exploratory missions will serve the same purpose for outer space.

By making spaceflight more affordable, more spaceflights can take place. That increase in activity will play a big role in ramping up public excitement about spaceflight because they will see something **actually being done** in space again, rather than seeing billions spent on a proposed big super rocket (called the *Space Launch System* or *SLS*) that may never be completed no matter how much money is thrown at it.

As you will see from specific real-world evidence presented herein, a number of NASA, university and industry studies have shown that we can return to the Moon and explore the inner solar system much sooner **with the budget we already have.** *We will also be able to economically exploit the vast potential of outer space as well.* How can this be done? By using **already-existing** commercial launch vehicles coupled with new technologies that are essentially already mature. Let's do that **instead of** continuing the **old expensive** Apollo paradigm that was **great** for beating the Russians to the Moon under a virtually **unlimited** budget in the 1960s, but is technologically and fiscally **obsolete** for doing both cutting-edge 21st century space exploration and economic exploitation without an unrelenting avalanche of inflowing money.

Thank you for taking the time to read this little soapbox speech. If you made it this far and have not completely dismissed what I have said out of hand, it is a testament to your objectivity and sense of fairness. As a scientist, I don't expect anyone to just take my word or anyone else's word in regard to the assertions stated in this book. That's the way science works: evidence is presented, but is accepted only after it has been scrutinized and verified many times in a number of different ways. Indeed, I would be skeptical in your position - - in fact I was initially *very* skeptical about most of the points I now profess as established fact in this tome. Given that fact, I will supply you with the third party source information I would want were I you: documented sources in the References section of this book that back my claims. References will be cited in the text by enclosing the surname of the author in parentheses for the referenced material along with the year of its publication. For instance, (Smith 2012) – not a real reference here. In the case of the same author having more than one cited work, his/her surname will be followed by a lower case letter that indicates the particular cited work. Example: (Jones a 2009) for the first work cited by Mr./Ms. Jones or (Jones b 2011) for the second. For multiple authors with the same surname, a number will be placed before the letter as in (Doe 1a 2012) for the first work of the first author whose last name is Doe and (Doe 2a 2012) for the first work of the second author named Doe. Those reading electronic editions of the book can click the citation and instantly be transported to the appropriate entry in the References section.

I also invite you to perform your own independent detailed researches to verify any of my contentions and to ascertain the validity of my sources. In science, minute scrutiny of one's work by others is quite literally the norm; therefore, that is what I always expect anyway, *so I urge you to pick apart everything I put forward rather than accept any point I state at face value.*

Finally, I hope to make the lay reader's experience more enjoyable by supplying simplified definitions of possibly unfamiliar scientific/technical jargon and acronyms within the Glossary of Space Terms. I may underline these terms either where they first appear in the book or at places so far removed from their first appearance that I think you may need to have your memory jogged. Those who are reading electronic editions of the book can click these underlined words to instantly be transported to the relevant definition in the glossary or an explanatory earlier part of the book. After all, even though it's rocket science, that doesn't mean I need to explain it in a manner that it is mind-blowing for any literate layperson who is not a scientist or engineer!

R.D. (Rick) Boozer, Master of Astronomy (in Astrophysics)
Astro Maven blog: **astromaven.blogspot.com**

Chapter 1: Learning the wrong lesson

"If you don't learn from your mistakes, then you're wasting some perfectly good mistakes!"
-- The author of this book to one of his physics students

The landing of the first humans on the Moon was one of the greatest events of history. If you are an American who was alive in the nineteen sixties, perhaps the proudest moment of your life occurred when Neil Armstrong and Buzz Aldrin first set foot on the Moon. I know it was for me, and it still is.

Figure 2: Saturn V Moon Rocket (Image Credit: NASA)

But as grand as that momentous event was, certain subsequent unrealistic ideas regarding how it should be interpreted have had a negative effect on U.S. spaceflight. I will explain what I mean by this statement shortly, but in the meantime I would ask the reader to keep one thought in mind that I will later back up with extensive evidence: the slowing of American progress in space over the last 40 years *was not* the fault of the monumentally historic Apollo program that landed men on the Moon or the talented people who made it happen. Instead, *it was due to Apollo being viewed through a distorting perceptual lens in its aftermath.* This grossly inaccurate *distortion* of the *meaning* of Apollo's great accomplishment has prevented us from living in a world where going to the Moon is routine and led to a world in which such flights are a capability currently lost to us. But honestly addressing the problem would mean a shifting of money and power from certain entities to which it has been going for a long time: a situation that some influential individuals and corporations would not tolerate. Once again, I remind the reader that corroborating evidence of the truth of this statement will be forthcoming in due course.

Those who are attempting to fix the situation are stepping on the vested interests of some powerful people and it is resistance from those same people which is the greatest problem holding back significant advancement of American spaceflight. Not insufficient funding for NASA (as some claim), but the wasting of funding that already exists. As you will see, if modern technology and methods are applied to the problem, we can send American astronauts on missions throughout the inner Solar System **without** greatly increasing NASA's budget.

Having stated the above premise, what specific *misinterpretations* of Project Apollo are holding us back and how are they being used by certain parties for temporary gain whilst ultimately weakening our country's space prowess?

Apollo was remarkably successful in its assigned task of **beating** the Russians to a manned Moon landing and **showing that the accomplishment was not a fluke** by repeating the feat a few times. A large super rocket was the **fastest** and **surest** way to meet that challenge given: 1) a **virtually unlimited** budget supplied from a sense of intense rivalry fueled by the Cold War between the U.S. and the Soviet Union, 2) the limited amount of time to accomplish the task set by President Kennedy, and 3) the state of rocketry and space technology in the 1960s. Indeed, that **was** the best way to beat the Russians in the *fastest* possible time with the essentially **unrestricted** budget that was available to NASA during that particular time period.

Unfortunately, after the success of Apollo, some people took the wrong lesson from it. Because Apollo got astronauts successfully to the

Moon and back by sending both the main spacecraft and the lunar lander together with all the propellant they needed in a launch on a gigantic hyper-expensive rocket, it was taken for granted from then on that that was *always the best* way to do space missions to the Moon and beyond. Ever since then, many sincere space exploration proponents (as well as some politicians seeking pork) have used that argument as a rationale for proposing large increases to NASA's human spaceflight budget; claiming such increases are necessary if America is to accomplish great feats in future human space exploration. For decades, I was among the many who thought an enormous hyper-expensive heavy lift rocket is *always* necessary to do any kind of ambitious human deep space flight; that is, until I finally saw extensive evidence (put forward by numerous innovative scientists and engineers of the highest credentials and repute) indicating the fallacy of this assumption.

Because the cost of each Saturn V rocket was proportional to its gargantuan size, numerous flights to the Moon were eventually considered unaffordable in the long run; leading to a limited number of flights and the cancellation of Project Apollo. So the irony is that the Apollo paradigm of a gigantic launch vehicle developed by the government is *not* the best way to *keep* going back to the Moon on an *indefinitely affordable* and *sustained* basis, particularly given technological advancements that have taken place in intervening decades. We continue to waste billions of dollars and precious human talent and time rather than learn from this "perfectly good mistake".

As I alluded in the Prologue to this book, studies completed by NASA, major universities, and industry have shown that there are more economically practical and sustainable methods for doing deep space flight. For the reader who doesn't want to wait until I discuss these studies in detail and who is comfortable with technical details, I suggest getting both some historical and technical background of these alternative methods with the following published research works: the NASA report titled *HAT Depot Requirements Study* (HSF 2011), the industry study from United Launch Alliance called *A Commercially Based Lunar Architecture* (Zegler, Cutter & Barr 2009), and the study from Georgia Tech and the National Institute of Aerospace known as *Near Term Space Exploration with Commercial Launch Vehicles Plus Propellant Depots* (Wilhite a et al. 2010). What you need to locate those and the many other expert studies that I will cite can be found in the References section of this book.

The three studies mentioned above were written either before the idea of SLS was put forward as written legislation or before its detailed specifications were formally published. Building upon these studies and bringing their contents up-to-date (via a direct extensive comparison of using the SLS in its latest proposed form versus using already existing launch vehicles) is another study from Georgia Tech called *Evolved Human Space Exploration Architecture Using Commercial Launch/Propellant Depots* (Wilhite b 2012).

For those readers that don't want to read through all of the technical details contained in the reports summarizing the above mentioned studies, I will be extensively condensing and describing those same studies in less technical terms throughout following pages.

But before we delve into the specifics of the professional studies, it is important to realize that the misconception of a gargantuan government-developed rocket being required for *all* types of human deep space exploration is not the sole conceptual aberration holding us back. That false idea is built on various prevalent myths leading to a general wrongheaded mindset that has kept us stuck in low Earth orbit for the past four decades instead of venturing back to the Moon and beyond to the planets. *Some* of these precepts were *actually true* many years ago, making their current acceptance seem more credible. Their earlier validity also makes it harder for people to shake free of them, especially those who haven't yet realized that the conditions under which the ideas held true no longer exist. Other ideas in this list of nearly holy canon were never really true, but instead are aberrations due to artificially induced conditions. These diehard false concepts are the topic of the following chapter.

Chapter 2: Common detrimental myths about spaceflight

"The greatest obstacle to discovery is not ignorance, but the illusion of knowledge."
-- *Daniel Boorstin, twelfth Librarian of Congress*

"You can see a lot just by looking."
-- *Yogi Berra*

Following is a list of common misconceptions concerning spaceflight that have persisted for a long while. Many of these incorrect concepts caused a retarding of our advancement into space for decades, primarily due to improper interpretation of the success of Apollo as described in the previous chapter.

Drawing from NASA, industry, and university studies, I will show that these "illusions of knowledge" are based on simplistic assumptions stemming from inspection of the facts at a relatively shallow level and that *looking at the issues more deeply* yields drastically different conclusions. I am listing these inaccurate ideas here to give a general overview of the issues you can expect to see covered in this book. After each myth, I will state a more accurate assessment for which I will offer substantial evidence in later pages. In the meantime, please keep an open mind and not rush to any snap decisions concerning any one of the counterclaims I present, even if it flies against everything you may have ever thought up to this point. Should you find yourself in such an incredulous situation, you should know that I was once in your shoes before I found out the relevant facts.

2.1 Myth: For ambitious exploration, NASA needs a large budget increase.

Significant human space exploration to the Moon, <u>asteroid</u> or <u>comet</u> bodies close to Earth (called <u>Near Earth Object</u>s or <u>NEO</u>s), and planets cannot occur unless NASA's budget is greatly increased.

Not so. The exorbitantly high cost of space travel over the decades has stemmed primarily from the economic and contractual structure under which NASA has been legally required to operate. This structure has hindered the use of more advanced technologies and alternate acquisition strategies that would have greatly reduced cost. A detailed discussion of those more practical technologies and acquisition strategies will be revealed as the reader progresses through this book.

As the former Executive Secretary of the NSC under the G.H.W. Bush administration mentioned, if we use those more up-to-date technologies and strategies *along with* cancelling SLS, then we can do *ambitious* deep space exploration projects with NASA's *current* budget. (Foust a 2012) What's more, many *notable* aerospace engineers and upper level managers from both the Apollo and Shuttle programs agree with him and the evidence supporting their positions will be supplied herein as well.

2.2 Myth: NASA designed and developed rockets are safer.

Because the people at NASA have decades of experience producing space transportation systems that the private commercial companies don't have, rockets and spacecraft designed and developed by NASA are probably safer than vehicles produced for the commercial market.

While it is true that personnel working for NASA and its traditional contractors are some of *the **best*** aerospace workers in the world, NASA does not have a monopoly on great rocket engineers and technicians. Here's something a lot of people may find a bit of a shocker: *No one **currently** working at NASA or its traditional contractors has designed and developed either a rocket for launching humans to orbit **or** a human crewed spacecraft that has **actually flown to orbit***. The engineers that actually worked on *design and development* of crewed spacecraft for NASA during the Mercury, Gemini, Apollo, and Shuttle programs have either retired and/or died. Furthermore, the best engineers in the commercial space market are top notch professionals who originally came from NASA and its usual contractor companies and who also work closely with NASA's best personnel during development of space vehicles for the commercial market. *Thus, the people who are designing and developing crewed spacecraft and launch vehicles for the commercial market have just as much experience in that field as the people now working for NASA and its traditional contractors.*

2.3 Myth: Shuttle-derived vehicles are safer.

New launch vehicles derived from Space Shuttle components are probably safer for launching astronauts than existing commercially

marketed launch vehicles with no heritage launching humans into space.

The entirely different physics involved in the flight characteristics of the Shuttle versus other vehicles means that the Shuttle's long used technologies will be employed in situations for which they were *not* originally designed. Worse, in most such cases the technologies have to be extensively modified to work in their new roles, thereby *increasing their costs and turning them into* **untried** *mechanisms with* **no** *safety track record!* A detailed specific example of this dilemma will be presented in the context of the next myth to be discussed.

2.4 Myth: Shuttle-derived vehicles are developed faster and cheaper.

New launch vehicles derived from Space Shuttle components for launching people into space can be developed faster and cheaper than they could be by using alternate technology because they are built from existing hardware and infrastructure that has been used to fly people to space for years.

Nope. See the immediately preceding statement concerning the safety of Shuttle-derived vehicles wherein it is pointed out that Shuttle technologies have to be extensively modified to such an extent that *essentially new* systems must be developed. A good example of this scenario is the now cancelled <u>*Ares-1*</u> launch vehicle that was originally proposed under the premise that it would use essentially an unmodified Shuttle booster for the main stage of the launch vehicle and a Shuttle main engine in the second stage; thereby, eliminating most of the development time and lowering costs because *it was thought* new technologies and support infrastructure would then be kept to a minimum. Instead, it turned out that the physical characteristics of an Ares-1 flight were *so different* from that of the Shuttle that: 1) an extensively modified 5 segment solid fuel rocket booster rather than the standard 4 segment Shuttle booster was needed, 2) a *new* shock absorber to get rid of vibrations of *unexpected* and *dangerous* severity had to be developed to protect a human crew, and 3) the Shuttle main engine could not be used because of the difficulty of modifying it to restart in flight (necessitating the development of an entirely new second stage engine derived from the Apollo Saturn J-2 engine). And all of those are just *a few* of the disadvantages encountered in the development of Ares-1 due to the inadequacy of Shuttle technology.

For instance, the final Ares-1 would have been able to launch a payload amount to orbit similar to that of <u>*Space Exploration Technologies' Falcon 9*</u>; however, a joint Air Force/NASA study concluded that if NASA had developed exactly the same Falcon 9 launcher as SpaceX did using normal

NASA procedures, then the total development costs of Falcon 9 would have been *at least* three times and *up to* eight times the total that SpaceX spent on their launcher. (NADAP 2011) Since Ares-1 was developed using the same NASA standard procedures that would have ballooned Falcon 9's development costs, that conclusion tells us that Ares-1 exorbitant budget overruns were not just due to unanticipated technical challenges. Specifics on this point will come in due course.

The up to eight times cheaper development estimate for Falcon 9 versus how much would have been spent by NASA is apparently not a fluke. Earlier a study was done of how SpaceHab developed two pressurized modules for use on the International Space Station. Price Waterhouse estimated that SpaceHab's development costs were also a factor of eight less than what could have been done following NASA's normal procedures. So there seems to be a trend here and it is one that is not necessarily the fault of NASA itself, but of externally set procedures that it is legally forced to use. (Miller 2012) Again details will be presented later in this book.

Figure 3: Falcon 9 launching cargo in Dragon spacecraft (Image credit: NASA)

More astounding is the fact that NASA got even more "bang for the buck" from SpaceX than the Air Force/NASA study would indicate. Around $9 billion was spent by NASA on the Orion spacecraft/Ares-1 launcher (Williams & Schatz 2010) up until the time Ares-1 was cancelled (the Orion spacecraft is still in development under the MPCV program). Had it not been terminated, it is estimated that just the Ares-1 launch vehicle *alone* would have cost *many more* billions of dollars to finish, as the last cited reference documents. Contrast that to the total amount that NASA actually paid SpaceX. *NASA only paid a fraction of the development costs for Dragon/Falcon 9 and SpaceX funded the rest.* In fact, the *total cost* paid by NASA to SpaceX of $336.7 million for the first three Falcon 9 flights (Ferster & Leone 2012) (which also included the cost of two Dragon pressurized cargo spacecraft) was less than what NASA paid for the construction of the launch tower for the Ares-1 launch pad!

But again, the reader needs to realize that the decisions that led to the Ares-1 fiasco were primarily political. *The fine engineers and personnel of NASA worked on what they were told to work on, not necessarily what they thought was optimal.* Unfortunately, a lot of the same faulty logic used to justify Ares-1 is now being used as an excuse for the current development of the launcher known as SLS, as will be shown later in this book.

2.5 Myth: Safety cannot be regulated too much.

Launchers and spacecraft for the commercial market need to be "man-rated" by NASA (in the extensive way that NASA rated rocket launchers for both the Mercury and Gemini programs in the 1960s) to insure they are safe for launching human beings into space. The reason why is that rockets from the commercial market are less reliable than vehicles that were designed and developed under extensive NASA control.

NASA does indeed need to closely scrutinize the safety of vehicles that are to transport America's astronauts to space. The problem is that some insist on going by the obsolete 1960s definition of "man-rated" that was necessary to the success of the early days of the U.S space program when launchers were notoriously unreliable (as in quite often blowing up at or just after liftoff) to the extent that NASA had no choice but to micromanage and dictate all aspects of safety features down to the manufacturing of the smallest nut and bolt.

Why did early launchers have such low reliability? The Atlas and Titan rockets (used in the Mercury and Gemini manned programs, respectively) were merely modified ICBMs. For their original purpose, it was acceptable for only two out three or even one out of three nuclear warheads to actually reach their target. Mass production and relatively simple operation were a higher priority to the military since many of the missiles would need to be assembled and put into operation at silos with small crews. Thus the need for NASA to implement *extreme* safety modifications on the early military launch vehicles.

Figure 4: Early Atlas rocket with Mercury spacecraft (Image credit: NASA)

Figure 5: Titan rocket launching Gemini spacecraft (Image credit: NASA)

However, safety requirements for flying people on *modern* and *more reliable* launch vehicles will not necessitate as extensive an amount of interventional oversight nor as much changing of hardware as was the case in the early days of the space program. A modern day technologically advanced Atlas V rocket is a *long, long* way from being the relatively primitive Atlas launch vehicle that sent John Glenn on the first American orbital flight while our whole nation kept its fingers crossed. That's the reason why the Air Force classifies Atlas V and Delta IV as *Evolved* Expendable Launch Vehicles to denote that they are *far more advanced* than their predecessors of earlier decades.

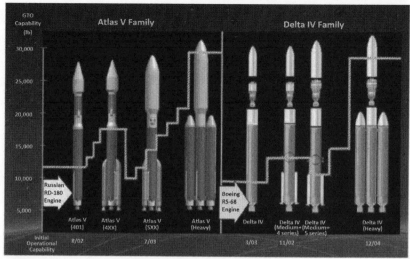

Figure 6: The modern Atlas V and Delta IV launcher families (Image Credit: AFSPC/PA)

Think about it, modern Atlas V and Delta IV launchers from _ULA_ have reliably launched satellites and robotic deep-space probes worth billions of dollars for many years for the Defense Department, NASA and large communication corporations. Many of the satellites are the space-based assets that our armed forces need in crucial life or death situations and are essential to our national security, as well as important key assets on which our nation's economy relies. Thus, reliability of the launch vehicles that put these assets where they need to be is of *truly vital* importance. Nowadays any company producing unreliable boosters rapidly finds themselves out of business because 1) insurance companies would refuse to underwrite the launch of payloads on their launchers, and 2) customers would not be willing to take the risk with their multi-billion dollar payloads. Given these facts, anyone who in honesty says modern commercial launchers have reliability issues has not taken the extensive time-consuming effort that is needed to keep up with the changes made in the industry in the intervening decades since the 1960s.

Does all of this mean that proven reliable satellite launchers (such as Atlas V and Delta IV) won't need *any* alterations to be ready for human flight? No, of course, not! Changes must be made because these vehicles were not originally designed for transporting living passengers. For one thing the flight path, fuel burn times, and maximum accelerations of the launch vehicle must be significantly changed from one typically used for launching satellites because of crew safety reasons. Furthermore, a few hardware modifications must be done to the launch vehicle (mainly in the form of added redundant sensors and automatic systems) that will constantly check for out of tolerance conditions dangerous to a human crew and make appropriate adjustments and warnings if needed. After all, your car is probably extremely reliable, but it still has such things as sensors for out of tolerance oil pressure, temperature, etc. along with automatic systems that try to keep safety tolerances from being exceeded.

The changes made to *modern* launch vehicles will be *minor* compared to the extensive alterations for correcting extreme unreliability that were made on earlier 1960s commercial launch vehicles when they were converted to allow Mercury and Gemini astronauts to fly with them. It was those fundamental reliability issues that were the original cause behind the creation of the "man-rated" concept. Since reliability is no longer as questionable an issue, the original purpose behind the "man-rating" concept does not apply. Meticulous safety checks of the vehicle done to a similar level to what is practiced in the manufacture and operational maintenance of passenger airliners should be quite adequate, *not* micromanaging by NASA of every tiny manufacturing step of each nut and bolt or flight readying procedure.

In the case of the Falcon 9 launch vehicle, SpaceX designed it to *far exceed* all of NASA's published human safety specifications *from the beginning*. For instance, NASA safety standards for astronaut flight dictate that structural integrity must be met to a tolerance of 125% of what is needed to give reasonable safety, but SpaceX *from the beginning* of the Falcon 9 program have not accepted less than 140% tolerance, whilst the same requirement will also apply to the Falcon Heavy. (Money a 2012) If there are any safety specifications that SpaceX have not implemented, it is because these specifications have not been published by NASA. However, no matter what, SpaceX should have to make few (if any) changes to their existing safety standards because of the extensive work *they have already done* in addressing that problem.

Given these circumstances, it is a good idea not to get NASA *too* involved with minutely controlling the designs of safety systems for Commercial Crew launchers and spacecraft. Why? Ironically, *excessive bureaucratically imposed safety procedures can actually lead to vehicles that are **less** safe*. A passage from a report summarizing a study done by the *Space Foundation*, a prominent nonprofit spaceflight issues think-tank, sums up the reasons for that situation very well (part of the text was boldfaced and underlined by the author of this book for emphasis):

> *"Bureaucracies usually try to mitigate risk by adding procedures and regulations to existing practices. This effort results in increased paperwork, overhead, and transaction costs that may ultimately outweigh the benefits of the regulation in the first place. For example, in the processing of the Space Shuttle's Solid Rocket Boosters, line workers proposed a procedural change*

that would speed up processing (and arguably make the process more reliable), but when they tried to introduce the change, they were told that it would be too expensive to change the applicable manuals and written procedures. The number of manuals and written procedures, in turn, arose from a desire to minimize risk by making sure everything is well documented. **NASA ended up with a time-consuming, (potentially) less safe procedure, as an indirect result of behaviors intended to ensure safety."** (Space Foundation 2012)

2.6 Myth: Build SLS or the Chinese will own space!

If we don't greatly accelerate the building of a large shuttle-derived heavy-lift launch vehicle called SLS by increasing its part of NASA's budget, the Chinese will beat us back to the Moon and completely dominate outer space.

In fact, I will put forward third-party evidence which indicates proceeding with SLS (either with higher financing or not) will actually *erode away* much of the considerable lead the U.S. has over China in human spaceflight.

2.7 Myth: Chemical powered rockets have to be expensive to fly.

Spaceflight cannot be made significantly cheaper than it historically has been as long as the conventional method of chemical propulsion is used.

Many naively claim that the classic *Rocket Equation* dictates that the extremely large mass of the launch vehicle (mostly propellant) at lift off compared to the relatively tiny amount of payload that will actually reach orbit can only result in exorbitant costs. *Though most of the mass of the launch vehicle/spacecraft combination is* **propellant;** *that enormous mass of propellant contributes* **far less than 1%** *of launch costs.* (Braconnier 2011) The reason why is because rocket propellant (fuel along with oxidizer needed to burn the fuel) is *cheap* compared to the development, construction and maintenance costs for a rocket. Indeed, a typical gallon of rocket propellant costs less than a gallon of milk! As I will later elucidate, most of the expense is due to ingrained practices of the industry and the economic effects of a certain type of legal contract that traditionally is mandated when NASA hires a company to do a project, not as a result of using conventional chemical propulsion. Also, the technology of in-space fill-up stations (called propellant depots) will lower the cost of leaving Low Earth Orbit (LEO); thereby, dropping overall costs even further. In short, we don't have to wait for nuclear rockets or some other alternate technology in order to

24

obtain more economically practical spaceflight. Again, a discussion of the proof of this assertion is coming. Though all of those factors by themselves will be enough to *greatly* lower costs of missions, another key advancement (touched upon in the discussion of Myth 12) would cause them to *plummet* even further.

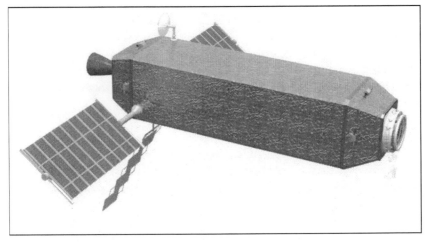

Figure 7: Proposed propellant depot (Image credit: NASA)

2.8 Myth: The Commercial Crew Program hinders space exploration.

The current emphasis on reducing the cost of getting people and materials into Earth orbit via the Commercial Crew program is *slowing down* our advance into the solar system. Only giving _high priority_ to the development of a giant super rocket derived from shuttle technology (such as SLS) will speed up the process.

The inverse is true; SLS will *slow down* the process of sending Americans back to the Moon and spreading our presence beyond; whilst efforts to reduce the cost to orbit will speed up our outward expansion. As an independent study (Booz-Allen-Hamilton 2011) commissioned by NASA indicates, it appears the costs of SLS probably won't be contained within its budget over the long haul; resulting in an indefinite extension of its development time -- an extension that would probably happen even if the budget for SLS was *substantially* increased. In contrast, lowering the cost of access to Earth orbit will speed up our spread through the solar system because a *major part* of the current expense of flights into deep space is just getting up from the ground to Earth orbit. *Before you can go anywhere else you have to get to Earth orbit first.* Thus, the cheaper the cost to Earth orbit, the more flights you can afford to go *anywhere* in the Solar System. Also, that means you have more money to spend on developing the spacecraft that is needed to get from LEO to your final destination. *The exorbitant cost of merely getting to orbit has been one of the primary reasons that we have not gone beyond LEO for the last forty years.*

In recent years, costs for access to LEO have been taking a *precipitous nose dive* (rather, the costs from *at least* one particular launch vehicle manufacturer have dropped drastically and others will have to follow suit or perish). This drop is due to certain recently occurring factors that I will cover in later pages. What's more, I will demonstrate that this significant downward trend in launch costs may well continue for years into the future.

2.9 Myth: Depots are useless unless they are restocked from the Moon.

The huge expense of hauling rocket propellant up from Earth to orbit means in-space refueling stations (known as *propellant depots*) _currently_ offer no cost and performance savings for deep spaceflight to the Moon and beyond. Depots will be an advantage _only_ after we can obtain propellant from the Moon or asteroids.

Not true for the same reason that it is an advantage for the Air Force to go to the extra expense of this process: hauling a large payload of fuel by tanker plane to a location far from where the loaded tanker took off and then transfer the fuel to a receiving plane that is in flight on a mission. Though the Air Force pays high operational costs and burns more fuel this way, it still is much cheaper and more practical than building and operating an enormously huge fighter or bomber big enough to hold all the fuel it needs for an entire round trip mission of up to 20,000 miles.

Yes, launches of medium sized rockets to send propellant to depots (from which spacecraft will top off their propellant tanks) located both in low Earth orbit and at L2[2] will cost money, as will the propellant itself. However, it won't cost nearly as much as building and operating an enormous launch vehicle that is huge enough to lift a cumbersomely massive and fully loaded spacecraft *in one launch* that: 1) contains enough propellant for a complete and *entire* deep space mission and 2) flies only a couple of times per year for a cost in excess of $1.5 billion per flight in the case of SLS. I know there are some more optimistic claims of $500 million per flight for SLS, but I'll point out other sources with solid evidence to the contrary.

---

[2] Never heard of L2? Consult the glossary of this book.

Instead, the same spacecraft can be launched with nearly empty propellant tanks on a much smaller already existing rocket since the spacecraft will be *much less heavy* without all that fuel. Once in orbit the spacecraft fills its propellant tanks from a depot in LEO before it proceeds on its trip to the Moon. Or, in the case of a mission to an asteroid, Mars, etc. there may be a stop at a way station at L2 or a rendezvous with a bigger spacecraft to take the crew deeper into unexplored space and on to the final destination.

In other words, we don't have to spend the billions needed to develop the proposed big launch vehicle to start doing ambitious missions. Even better, we won't have to wait year after year for SLS to be built so that we can begin the great adventure of spreading Americans throughout the inner Solar System. We can get started *now*!

2.10 Myth: Space stations and depots require heavy lift rockets.
The building of *large* space stations and propellant depots is *currently* not practical, because completion of these structures would require a large heavy-lift launch vehicle to lift the depot's massive components.

Using existing medium-lift launch vehicles for this purpose would only require a somewhat different design for in-orbit assembly of modules constructed from parts sent up with more launches of those existing medium sized rockets. In short, it would involve leveraging the lessons we learned and the technologies we developed from assembling ISS in orbit. The greater number of launches of medium sized vehicles would still cost far less and be more reliable than the required smaller number of SLS launches for reasons that will be explained. In fact, with a large HLV such as SLS, there would be a greater risk to the project on each single launch, and the loss of a hyper-expensive HLV in a mishap means an even heavier cost (in both funds and time) to replace it. On the other hand, with a smaller rocket a smaller fraction of valuable payload is risked with each launch. What's more, these more common launchers *are already manufactured* in *significant numbers* for the commercial market, meaning the *much lower* replacement cost of such a launcher wouldn't do as much harm to the project's budget in the event of a bad launch.

2.11 Myth: Human space flight must hurt robotic space exploration.
The relationship between human spaceflight and robotic space exploration is naturally antagonistic. Either can only be done at the expense and detriment of the other.

Remember the current high cost of getting to orbit is a large fraction of any mission cost. If the cost of accessing space is greatly reduced, the cost of launching either type of exploration will be correspondingly reduced. The end result is a situation where money is not as likely to be taken from a project just to be able to afford launching a mission belonging to another project (as is the norm now).

2.12 Myth: Reusable rockets don't save money.
The Space Shuttle _proved_ that a reusable chemically powered launch vehicle offers _no savings_ in cost and efficiency over single-launch expendable launch vehicles.

False because a) the Shuttle was not *fully* reusable by a long shot and b) the gargantuan expense of maintaining the *enormous* standing army of personnel spread across the country that it took to launch and maintain the Shuttle. In conjunction with the addressing of issues touched upon in regard to Myth 7, reusability will be the big game changer that will allow *truly* low cost access to space. Be patient, proof will follow.

2.13 Myth: Russians are hauling Americans to ISS because of Obama.
The decision that the Russians would be the only means of flying American astronauts into space for years (until new American space vehicles were available to replace the Space Shuttle for ferrying crew) was made during the Obama administration.

Not true. That policy was instituted and the first contracts signed with the Russians during the G.W. Bush administration. But this was a sensible move that should not be condemned no matter which administration was responsible. After a new NASA administrator was appointed during the G.W. Bush administration, that administrator decided to develop the Ares 1 launcher and Orion spacecraft rather than go with an alternately proposed option that was similar to the now existing Commercial Crew program (despite recommendations for the latter option expressed by the Associate Administrator for Exploration Systems (Foust g)). During that time it was recognized that, even under the most optimistic projections, no new vehicles would be ready until *years* after the Space Shuttle fleet was retired. At that point it was decided to rely solely on the Russians. So even if Ares-1 had not been cancelled, American astronauts would still be flying on Russian vehicles. As it turns out, it appears that new American vehicles will be available for crewed flight around the time that Ares-1/Orion was *originally* scheduled to be finished. However, as is now known, Ares-

1/Orion could never have been finished even close to its originally slated time table, but many years afterward at best.

Figure 8: Russian Soyuz spacecraft bringing passengers to ISS (Image credit: NASA)

2.14 Myth: The G.W. Bush administration messed up the Shuttle.

The G.W. Bush administration didn't need to contract the Russians to transport our astronauts to the ISS; instead, we should have continued Shuttle flights until alternative American launchers and spacecraft were available.

This myth has been perpetrated by people other than the ones who have spread the myth immediately preceding this one. It is just as unfair to blame the Bush administration in this regard as it is to blame the Obama administration for the other situation. Shuttles were so expensive to operate that they would have consumed too much of the money needed for the development of the new vehicles and technologies needed to replace them. Furthermore, both the Challenger and Columbia accidents showed that we need launch vehicles and spacecraft less vulnerable to fatal mishap than the Shuttle.

Figure 9: A Space Shuttle launch (Image credit: NASA)

2.15 Myth: Relying on Russia never happened before.

Before the retirement of the Shuttle, the United States had never had to *totally* rely on another country to ferry our astronauts to the International Space Station.

Again, not true. For two years after the Columbia accident, the Space Shuttle was in disuse while the accident was thoroughly investigated. During that period, all American astronauts sent to the ISS went on Russian vehicles just as is happening now.

2.16 Myth: All NASA launchers and spacecraft are "commercial" vehicles.

NASA does <u>not</u> *actually build* launchers and spacecraft, but instead relies on companies in the private aerospace industry. Thus, all of vehicles produced by NASA are "commercial" and there is nothing new about current so-called "commercial" launchers and spacecraft.

NASA does *indeed* build launchers and spacecraft from the standpoint that they design new vehicles and then minutely supervise development of those vehicles whilst their private industry contractors work on them. This situation is analogous to a housing contractor being said to *build* a home even though he may contract out the *actual assembly* of the structure to one company, the electrical wiring to another, the plumbing to yet another company, and so on. NASA was intensively involved in the design and development of both the Saturn V moon rocket and the Space Shuttle, just as they currently are with both SLS and Orion-MPCV; therefore, NASA can *truthfully* be said to be a builder of rockets and spacecraft.

Furthermore, *none* of those vehicles are designed to compete in the commercial market for launching communications satellites, GPS satellites, space tourists, etc.; therefore, they are NOT commercial vehicles.

Contrast that way of doing things to the direction exemplified by the true commercial market space vehicles. Though these companies may get *part* of their vehicle development financed by NASA as a way of insuring that the space agency doesn't waste money reinventing the wheel (so to speak), NASA also helps spur the industry forward by doing so because the companies producing these vehicles will use them for purposes *far beyond* the needs of NASA or the Air Force. These vehicles will get used for all of the commercial market purposes that I mentioned in the previous paragraph and more. Given this fact, they are *true* commercial vehicles.

I finish this chapter by reminding the reader once more that corroborating evidence will be revealed from professional studies supporting all of the assertions I have made up to this point and any other assertions I will make later.

Chapter 3: The paradox of SLS

Alice laughed: "There's no use trying," she said; "one can't believe impossible things."
"I daresay you haven't had much practice," said the Queen. "When I was younger, I
always did it for half an hour a day. Why, sometimes I've believed as many as six
impossible things before breakfast."
        -- Lewis Carroll – from Alice's Adventures in Wonderland

"For a successful technology, reality must take precedence over public relations, for nature
cannot be fooled."
        -- Richard Feynman – Nobel Prize winning physicist - from *Report to*
        the Space Shuttle Challenger Inquiry

"An elephant: a mouse designed to government specifications."
        -- Robert Heinlein – from Excerpts from the Notebooks of Lazarus Long

Perhaps the biggest current threat to American preeminence in outer space is the spending of a significant fraction of the NASA budget on a rocket that is officially termed the *Space Launch System* or *SLS* for short. As I will show, that assessment is the view of such notables as the legendary *Christopher Kraft* (a leading NASA engineer and manager until the Apollo moon landings and later Director of the Johnson Space Center), *Tom Moser* (former director of Johnson Space Center Engineering, and former director of NASA's Space Station Program), *Robert Walker* (former chairman of the House Science and Technology Committee), *Charles Miller* (former NASA senior adviser for commercial space) and *Buzz Aldrin* (the second person to set foot on the Moon and inventor of the innovative Aldrin *Mars Cycler* concept that is minimally defined in the glossary of this book). I am listing these particular gentlemen just for *starters*, since I will be spotlighting many more prominent space industry figures with critical assessments of SLS. Yet proponents of this vehicle claim it is a way to preserve our country's space leadership. How did the latter situation of what I call "White Queen thought processes" become dominant?

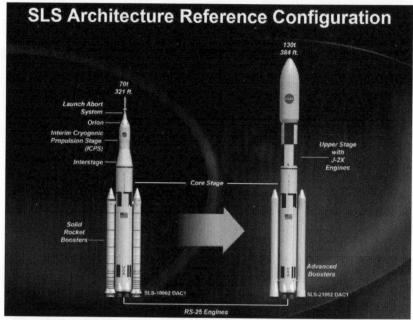

Figure 10: Proposed smaller and larger versions of SLS (Image credit: NASA)

3.1 The genesis of SLS

Heavily influenced by the findings of the Augustine Committee, the main space-related goal sought by the Obama administration after cancelling Ares-1 was to hand the transport of American astronauts to the space station over to independent commercial launch vehicle/spacecraft producers and to end reliance for this service by the Russians as soon as possible. As was also stated in their original plan, another objective was the development of a large heavy lift vehicle for deep space exploration. However, that vehicle was to be developed via competition between commercial companies and by employing newer more advanced technologies, both of which should have made the launcher more efficient and cost effective than previous large launchers as well as safer. This situation was not to the liking of Senators and Congresspersons representing constituencies where a large number of people had jobs related to the Space Shuttle. Their chagrin stemmed from the fact that worker's skills and factory facilities used with the older Space Shuttle technology would not be applicable to the new HLV project. In short, many of their constituents who were employed maintaining the Shuttle would be out of jobs.

Thus, a group of Senators (from states that had previously gotten significant economic benefits from Space Shuttle) came up with SLS as a bargaining chip to use in negotiations with the Obama administration. Their idea was to effectively resurrect the Ares-V heavy-lift launch vehicle that was cancelled at the same time Ares-1 was brought to a halt when Project Constellation was killed. Ares-V was originally slated to launch the fully fueled spacecraft, service module and lunar lander for a trip to the Moon, whilst Ares-1 was to launch the crew in the Orion space capsule for a rendezvous with that large vehicle combination waiting for them in orbit. One might paraphrase the Senators' position put forth to the Obama administration as, "OK, you want to hand over crew launching operations for the International Space Station to privately operated commercial concerns. We'll go along *if* you will accept NASA developing a large rocket using *existing* Shuttle technology and thus employ large numbers of our constituents that were previously employed in the Shuttle program." This is how SLS came to be derogatorily referred to by many as the "Senate Launch System".

By-the-way, even before the SLS deal, it was decided that development of the Orion spacecraft was to continue after the death of its parent Constellation moon-return program. Orion was a major cash cow for certain political constituencies and was to be part of a bigger spacecraft called *MPCV* for *Multi-Purpose Crew Vehicle*. Or perhaps a more apt acronym for it is the one given by its detractors: *More Politically Correct Vehicle*. More on this later, but for now, we go back to the machinations behind the creation of the SLS project.

Seeing that winning a significant part of the battle was better than getting nothing at all, the Administration accepted the Senators' offer in order to get a reliable and more budget friendly commercial spaceflight industry going as soon as possible that would end our embarrassing reliance on the Russians. Furthermore, it was also hoped that the lowering of launch costs commensurate with the Commercial Crew effort would stimulate a new private human spaceflight industry that would ultimately be a great stimulus to the U.S. economy and foster American scientific and technological leadership for generations to come.

Thus, the country's future in space was held for ransom for the short-term economic advantage of those states traditionally associated with the Space Shuttle.

3.2 The gorging on SLS pork begins

In fact Senator Orin Hatch of Utah actually *bragged* that he had put a specification into the requirements for SLS such that NASA would be *forced* to use solid rocket boosters built in Utah by ATK! The following two paragraphs in italics are literally quoted from *The Mainstreet Business Journal* (Eddington 2010)

> *"Sen. Orrin Hatch (R-Utah) said, "Though we will have hurdles to face in the future, the House passage of the Senate bill builds a foundation for the future of the civilian solid rocket motor industry in Utah," Hatch said. "This was a collaborative effort, and I'm grateful to members of the Utah congressional delegation for their hard work and support on this legislation."*
> *Hatch was successful in getting language inserted in the bill which details specific payload requirements for a heavy-lift space launch system that, Utah industry experts agree, can only be realistically met through the use of solid rocket motors like the ones manufactured by ATK in northern Utah. The legislation further requires NASA to use, to the extent practicable, existing contracts, workforces and industries from the Space Shuttle and Ares rockets, including solid rocket motors."* (Eddington 2010)

To emphasize that jobs within certain constituencies was the primary motivator (rather than what was best for advancing our overall national space effort forward), following are quotes from other Senators who were instrumental to the instigation of SLS.

A significant player in the creation of the SLS project was Senator Bill Nelson of Florida, who said, *"... the government's financial commitment over the next five to six years would be about $18 billion – $10bn for the rocket, $6bn for the multi-purpose crew vehicle salvaged from the axed Constellation programme, and **a further $2bn to be spent on ground support and developing launch facilities at Florida's Kennedy Space Centre."*** (Luscombe 2011) Boldfaced emphasis was added by the author of this book to draw attention to what was most advantageous to the good Senator.

Senator Kay Bailey Hutchinson of Texas, who NASA administrator Charlie Bolden has referred to as the "Queen Bee" behind the creation of the bill that begat the SLS project, issued this statement:

> *"This bill provides needed direction to NASA that will preserve many of the jobs and critical skills the agency would continue to lose amid budgetary uncertainty."* (King 2010)

Recall the earlier mentioned independent study that NASA commissioned concerning SLS. In a most ironic public statement, Ms. Hutchinson *partially* quoted a key statement from the study's final report in a way that made it *sound* as if the report *endorsed* SLS when, as I stated earlier, it did not. She essentially said the study's statement that SLS would stay within budget for 3 to 5 years (Booz-Allen-Hamilton 2011) was a reason for NASA not to resist starting the construction of SLS. However, Ms. Hutchinson neglected to include the part where the study mentions that after that time period the development project would likely blow its budget and not be completed for that reason. (Cowing a 2011) *In other words, the study states that what ended up killing Ares-1 is likely to ultimately kill SLS.* Apparently, Ms Hutchison is as much "White Queen" as she is "Queen Bee".

An article in one Florida newspaper offered perhaps a very straight forward evaluation of the bill that created SLS:

> *"The intent of the law, championed by U.S. Sens. Bill Nelson, D-Fla., and Kay Bailey Hutchison, R-Texas, was to keep shuttle contractors in business while preserving at least some of the shuttle jobs in Florida, Texas and elsewhere that are set to go away after the [Shuttle] orbiter's last flight."* (Matthews a 2011)

Stated differently, many of those "jobs" and "skills" (to which Senator Hutchinson referred) are "critical" *only* if a *Shuttle-derived* heavy-lift vehicle is considered the most effective way to perform deep space operations. But this assertion has been refuted by a number of studies that I have already mentioned which were done by NASA, industry and scientific academia. Later, in-depth coverage of these studies within the pages of this book will bolster that argument even more strongly.

In effect, the good Senators told the rocket engineers who were to build the new rocket that the implementation of the engineers' designs would be **restricted** *to a suite of* **existing** *technologies and architectures for which there was significant infrastructure in the Senators' states.* The primary idea was to make the project as big as possible to employ the maximum number of the Senators' constituents, with actual end-product usefulness being a secondary concern at best. Senators designing rockets! Stated slightly differently, SLS is the real world manifestation of Mr. Heinlein's "elephant".

Sadly for Senator Hatch, it appears his meticulously constructed requirements will not exclude competitors of ATK after all. Senator Richard Shelby of Alabama is another significant backer of SLS, but he has done an about-face in regards to using ATK solid rocket boosters on the launcher. As stated earlier, ATK solid rocket boosters are made in Utah, but after the bill instigating SLS was passed, *Teledyne Brown Engineering* and *Aerojet* proposed an alternative booster that could be produced in Alabama of which Mr. Shelby has expressed some enthusiasm for obvious reasons. (Messier a 2011) Evidently, in pork politics, it's the classic "every man for himself" situation regardless of any earlier understanding made between the politicians involved.

Thus, now only the initial smaller version of SLS *explicitly* includes ATK solid rocket boosters, whilst the larger version's boosters are ambiguously labeled "advanced boosters" until such time it is decided what company is to supply the boosters for that version. The reason for this nonspecific terminology change is that ATK now wants to submit an "upgraded" version of its SRB in response to the new competition from the builders of the so called "advanced" liquid propellant booster. I will speak in more detail about the proposed new SRB later.

Bragging seems to be a fundamental characteristic of pro-SLS Senators, because Mr. Shelby crowed to his constituents about being one of the primary proposers of a Continuing Resolution in 2011 that was intended to bolster the huge rocket. That resolution specified *in writing* that a large amount of the money in the SLS budget for 2011 would go to the Marshall Spaceflight Center in Huntsville, Alabama. A reporter at a newspaper in Decatur, Alabama noted the hypocrisy between Shelby's desire for pork and his professed Tea Party ideals:

> *"The fiscal 2011 budget vote made clear that tea party favorites ignore tea party principles once in power.*
> *U.S. Sen. Richard Shelby, R-Tuscaloosa, who rarely misses an opportunity to court the tea party, shot out a press release moments after the Senate passed the budget. Shelby "announced that he has successfully added language to the final Continuing Resolution for 2011 that requires NASA to fully develop its heavy lift capability. Through this addition, Sen. Shelby has saved hundreds of jobs at Marshall Space Flight Center."*
> *The budget language he added specifies that Marshall should spend $1.8 billion to build a rocket with a 130-ton lift capacity. The mission for which this rocket will be used remains unknown, and of course that's not the point.*
> *In a separate release the same day, Shelby announced his conservative voting record won him the "Taxpayers' Friend Award." A clue to his award may be that he voted against the same 2011 budget that he amended for Marshall's benefit."* (Fleischauer 2011)

Those are just *some* of the questionable activities of Richard Shelby, as we will see in a later chapter.

But let us return to the general issue of SLS existing primarily as a pork generator . . .

Some would say, "Well, so what? There is some element of pork politics involved in *any* project in which Congressional representatives become entangled. If SLS does what it is claimed to do and it advances America's leadership in the space frontier, that's OK." However, I will cite professional research and third-party evidence that, despite the claims of its proponents, *the **only** advantage of SLS is the above mentioned jobs going to the constituencies of certain politicians and it is **harmful** to the advancement of our country as a whole in the realm of 21st century space science and technology.*

3.3 The call for more practical alternatives to SLS

Perhaps of all the SLS critics, none are more experienced and knowledgeable than the earlier mentioned NASA luminaries *Chris Kraft* and *Tom Moser*, both of whom were key engineers involved in developing the hardware that transported the Apollo astronauts safely to the Moon and back. There are definitely no more articulate or better qualified spokesmen on the shortcomings of the expensive gargantuan SLS launcher than these two brilliant rocket scientists.

In the April 20, 2012 issue of the *Houston Chronicle*, Kraft and Moser laid out their case against the SLS. They stated that because of the exorbitant costs associated with SLS that:

"… the human deep space exploration program is on the verge of collapse".

More specifically they state:

"The SLS-based strategy is unaffordable, by definition, since the costs of developing, let alone operating, the SLS within a fixed or declining budget has crowded out funding for critical elements needed for any real deep space human exploration program." (Kraft & Moser 2012)

The gist of the previous paragraph is essentially that Congress has put NASA in the untenable position of building a rocket that would be useless because the large massive payloads it is designed to lift will not exist when the rocket is finished. Why would the payloads not exist? Because of the rocket's huge development cost taking money away from payload development! Furthermore, even were it to be finished and actually put to use, SLS would still siphon large amounts from other projects because of extraordinarily high operating costs. This fact has led to another dubious honor for SLS, being often referred to as: "The Rocket to Nowhere". White Queen thought processes indeed!

In other words, a finished SLS would be the spaceflight equivalent of the old joke about an atheist at his funeral: according to the beliefs he held in life, he was all dressed up with nowhere to go. So SLS is a very expensive solution looking for a yet-to-be-determined problem it can solve.

As Kraft and Moser further explain in the aforementioned article, a large heavy lift vehicle is *not* necessary for the type of deep space missions that SLS is supposed to launch. Instead, they make the point that I spoke of earlier about the greater practicality of sending up large parts on separate launches and assembling them in orbit by way of existing medium size launch vehicles.

Furthermore, those who peruse the previously cited Kraft and Moser article will discover something else interesting. They literally state and provide evidence to the effect that SLS will not bring significant benefits to Texas and especially the Houston area with its Manned Space Center. It appears Ms. Hutchison was very naïve in her support of the project.

In an article for the Wall Street Journal, former House Science and Technology Committee Chairman *Robert Walker* and former NASA Senior Adviser for Commercial Space *Charles Miller* echoed the criticism of Messrs. Kraft and Moser:

> *"Congress, and considerations about constituents in affected states such as Florida and Alabama, later stopped Mr. Obama's plan to cancel the government's super-heavy-lift rocket, which was known as Ares V and then recreated as the Space Launch System. But the president had showed boldness in trusting America's future to commercial companies.*
> *... Private industry can build the rockets, and do a much better job at lowering costs than any government agency. NASA can then focus on the important and difficult jobs that only NASA can do. Among other things, this would include developing game changing technologies such as advanced electric propulsion that are still too risky for any company to invest in, and which will create brand-new industries in the 21st century."* (Walker and Miller 2013)

Another critical voice to be considered is the only one of the Apollo astronauts who truly has PhD level credentials as a "rocket scientist". As Doctor Edwin (Buzz) Aldrin states:

> *"... we already have a fairly robust set of launch vehicles being provided by the commercial sector. So, in this area, we do not need the government competing to develop another launch vehicle. One could -- on another day -- even discuss whether we need a 130 metric ton launch vehicle, but assuming we do, the U.S. launch industry is capable of building a vehicle capable of such lift reasonably soon. After all, only four years were needed for the U.S. space launch industry to develop EELV. Likewise, Falcon 9 was developed in a little more than seven years.*
> *No, NASA's role is more important than simple lift to orbit. NASA needs to focus on the things that are really important, and that we do not know how to do. The agency is a pioneering force, and that is where its competitive advantage lies."* (Aldrin a 2012)

Dr. Aldrin's skepticism is echoed by former Space Shuttle astronaut Scott Parazynski., who spoke of SLS as follows:

> *"I worry about this one, in particular, because there's really not a destination with milestones," he said. "When you have a rocket, but you don't really know*

where it's going to take you yet, that becomes discretionary funding that's easily canceled. And that's what I think is going to happen." (Berger 2012)

The high cost of SLS is not just a detriment to the development of *human* deep space exploration/exploitation, but it also saps resources for endeavors such as the great *robotic* interplanetary explorations to Mars, Jupiter, Venus, Mercury, the Asteroid Belt, etc as well as orbiting astronomical observatories. Perhaps nothing expresses this dual dilemma better than the following excerpts from an open letter written to Congress from The Planetary Society. (Anderson 1a 2011)

"The Planetary Society is deeply troubled with the direction the agency is headed in and the wrong-headed decisions that are driving the human spaceflight program into the ground.

We are particularly upset with the cuts to NASA funding proposed by the House Appropriations Committee. While we all recognize the fiscal and economic challenges the nation faces, we believe the proposed cuts reflect perverse priorities and are too far reaching, in particular the proposed termination of the James Webb Space Telescope and cuts to Earth Science.

Most disturbing is that cuts to world-class science are being used to pay for increases to develop a new rocket -- the Space Launch System (SLS) -- that has no mission goals, that NASA cannot afford to build, that will not advance exploration.

With the intense fiscal pressure facing all agencies, NASA should focus on making the most efficient use of the money allocated to it. This means setting priorities and making decisions based on merit and readiness. It will be painful, but it is necessary. Most importantly, it is time to put wasteful programs aside, such as the SLS. We can no longer afford it, and it's an abuse of the agency's mission.

Those are strong words, but it's time to call out the strongest weapons we have in this fight to save our future in space. We've got to stand up to the narrow, parochial interests that are forcing NASA to build a rocket it doesn't want -- because neither the U.S. Congress nor the Administration has defined a mission for it.

This rocket to nowhere is inflicting painful damage on other NASA programs -- you'll see science -- both earth and planetary -- cut again. The new technology program that was to create the means to explore space more efficiently and more effectively will take a devastating hit. And the funds to jump-start a commercial rocket industry that could provide the long-sought affordable access to space were cut in half."

It doesn't take a Nobel Prize winning scientist like Dr. Feynman to see that here we have a situation where the public relations efforts of a few politicians are taking precedence over what objective reality dictates.

The reader may wonder: What is *"The new technology program that was to create the means to explore space more efficiently"* to which the Planetary Society letter refers and which suffers because of SLS? That is a very important question indeed and will be covered here in another chapter of this book.

3.4 The hypocrisy of some SLS supporters

In group discussions online, I occasionally encounter some of the more fanatical SLS proponents who claim to have a solution to the problem of not having the budget for payloads to loft on the giant rocket. They want to deorbit the International Space Station and divert the $3 billion per year that NASA spends on ISS to fund those payloads. If the other countries who are participating in the ISS program don't like their extensive investment in time, money and manpower being splashed into the Pacific Ocean, well "C'est la vie!"

Of course, while our relations with other countries are important, there would be other serious detrimental side effects to nixing ISS. According to SLS pushers, their favorite launch vehicle is to be America's primary means of returning to Moon and on to farther destinations such as an asteroid or Mars. But we currently haven't even started building a lander for Moon missions, and furthermore, many of the technologies needed to allow safe travel during the months-long journeys to destinations beyond the Moon have yet to be developed. One of the primary current uses of ISS is to help develop those needed technologies.

For example, one of the worst problems that will face astronauts on long journeys into deep space (that SLS would supposedly make possible) is a remedy to the extensive bone loss that occurs when the human body is exposed to weightlessness for long periods of time. The ISS is the only adequately accessible facility we have where the necessary long periods of weightlessness exist for experiments needed to find the answer to that problem.

Another technology that is due to be tested at ISS has the potential to shorten each leg of a round trip to Mars from 9 months to 39 days! It is an engine technology known as *VASIMR* (*VAriable Specific Impulse Magnetoplasma Rocket*) developed by former Space Shuttle astronaut *Franklin Chang-Diaz* under the auspices of his *Ad Astra Rocket Company*. An actual working prototype of this engine is to be extensively tested while it performs the function of boosting ISS's orbit to a higher altitude on occasions when the station's altitude becomes too low because of orbital decay. Of course, without the ISS there would be no massive structure existing for long enough times in space to adequately test this new state-of-the-art engine.

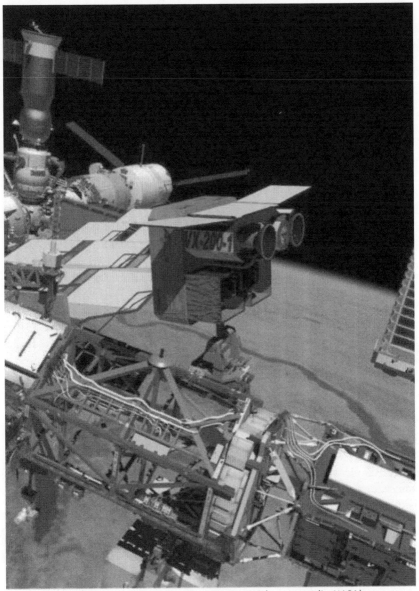

Figure 11: Proposed VASIMR engine on ISS (Image credit: NASA)

Also, how will living in the partial gravity of the Moon or Mars for extended periods of time affect the human body? We can find that out by producing a rotating module attached to the ISS that will give "artificial gravity" that is equivalent to the gravitational pull on the surface of the Moon or Mars and there are proposed plans for adding such a module.

All of the above examples are just a drop in the bucket as far as uses of the ISS for advancing the technologies needed to safely allow the deep space missions that SLS is supposed to facilitate. So getting rid of ISS to pay for spaceships to be lofted by SLS on deep space missions, but not knowing what the dangers of those missions are (because we didn't extensively test for them on the ISS) is shear foolhardiness.

In short, some SLS proponents belong to a faction that wants to get rid of the very laboratory that is required for us to determine the dangers of extensive spaceflight and the solutions needed to obviate those dangers when, ironically, their favorite launch vehicle is supposed to *enable* such flights.

3.5 Robbing Peter to pay Paul

It gets worse. SLS has been a real threat to the Commercial Crew program, whose purpose is to end our reliance on the Russians for carrying Americans to the International Space Station. In fact it may already be significantly delaying the date that the new American ferrying service will begin. For example, in NASA's 2011 budget proposed by the Obama administration, Commercial Crew was allocated at $850 million, but Congressional proponents of SLS finagled that amount down to $406 million, adding the difference to the budget for SLS. It is estimated that this could add another year of U.S. dependence on the Russians to ferry American astronauts to ISS; thereby, extending that date from 2016 to 2017. (Clark a 2011) So in transferring that money to SLS, they may have increased the amount of money that the American taxpayer will ultimately have to pay the Russians. That is money that could be going to *American* companies like ULA, SpaceX, Boeing, Sierra Nevada, etc. for crew transport on American spacecraft.

They also cut the amount for Commercial Crew requested by the administration's proposed 2012 NASA budget and put it "you know where". But that's not all. The Congressional personages responsible for this axing were able to negotiate a situation where the number of companies being paid by NASA to develop crew transport got cut from four down to two highly funded with a third having greatly reduced funding. Again, the reason for this downsizing was to have more money to put into SLS. An explanation of the importance of having as many *different* crewed vehicles as possible is another topic for later discussion.

However, in the time since the abovementioned "rob Peter to pay Paul" actions happened, a sort of compromise has been reached between pro-SLS and pro-Commercial Crew factions. An amendment (S.3661) was made to the Space Exploration Sustainability Act of 2013 that states that *neither* SLS development *nor* Commercial Crew development can have money removed from one's budget to pay for the other. So SLS cannot take money from Commercial Crew or vice versa. This means that if NASA's budget is cut for any reason or SLS runs over its budget, money to sustain SLS at its current level of funding would have to be cut from NASA programs *other than* Commercial Crew (for reasons I will cover later, it is literally *impossible* for Commercial Crew to go over budget). It appears that the recent successes of SpaceX have made it increasingly difficult for the Senators to plausibly continue to transfer Commercial Crew funding for their pet monster rocket. Thus, Senators Nelson and Hutchison included this new protective umbrella for Commercial Crew in the amendment.

3.6 Evidence that SLS is not practical

OK then, if SLS is definitely **not** a *practical* and *affordable* way to start spreading America's presence throughout the inner Solar System, then what is the evidence that this is the case? In the next couple of chapters I will discuss why its innate characteristics make it so expensive. I will also talk about how other launch vehicles (that *already* exist and are *currently* flying) can give us just as much *or more* spacefaring capability, greater flexibility of use, require *far less* financial outlay and without our waiting year-after-year for a flight-ready SLS *that may* **never** *come*.

Chapter 4: Why is SLS outrageously expensive compared to alternatives?

"You don't always get what you pay for, but you always pay for what you get."
-- anonymous

"The laws of Economics are as inescapable as the laws of Physics."
-- The author of this book addressing a supporter of SLS

As has already been indicated, the total development costs of SLS are so high it will probably never be finished. Also, even if it could be completed, the cost per flight would be so prohibitively expensive that we could not afford to launch it more than two or three times per year. That is the reason why when you hear proponents of SLS espouse what they consider the virtues of their beloved launcher, they will usually behave as though its cost is irrelevant and instead concentrate on its proposed technical capabilities. If forced to face economic issues in a discussion of SLS, such a person will typically cite only a *part* of its expense as though it is the *entire* expense (either through innocent misconceptions or purposeful deceit, depending on the individual), as will be pointed out in detail in this very chapter. As mentioned earlier, studies conducted by NASA, industry, and universities show that some of the missions in which an SLS sized launcher would be used could be done sooner, more effectively and safer with multiple launches of medium-sized vehicles. But due to a genuine lack of knowledge of that fact or a purposeful non-acknowledgement, an SLS advocate may behave as if those studies don't exist.

Furthermore, *if* there ever is a situation where it is deemed a super HLV is needed for a particular deep space mission, other possible alternative HLVs offer equivalent or *even greater* lift capacity and safety than SLS and could be produced for *much less cost* within a *shorter time span*. Evidence for this assertion is coming. No matter what, the salient point is that important NASA projects end up losing part or all of their funding as a consequence of the high costs of SLS and/or the misrepresentation of those costs.

What are the causes behind such exorbitant SLS development and operational costs?

4.1 Cost-plus contracting and FAR

A system called "cost-plus contracting" is a primary player in making SLS a money devouring fiscal black hole that will not be sustainable in the long run. No better real-world example exists of the negative effects of cost-plus contracting than the events leading to the cancellation of the Ares-1 booster that was part of NASA's Project Constellation. A brief look into the plight of that ill-fated project may give us some insight into similar pitfalls that await SLS.

When cost-plus contracting is employed, NASA pays **all** of the costs of developing a vehicle plus a percentage above the cost (for example, the contractor's cost and 10% above that) and the contracted company or companies get paid for these development costs whether they produce *successfully* working hardware or not. Do you see the problem here? Whether or not anything *useful* is produced, the contractor still receives *full* payment. ***In other words, failure gets rewarded and there is not a lot of incentive to get things done on time or within budget!***

Before proceeding further, it should be pointed out that there are situations where cost-plus contracting is actually *advantageous*. This approach makes sense at the start of *some* Research and Development projects where the total cost cannot be determined ahead of time because of the unanticipated problems that often arise when developing *radically new* technologies. Cost-plus was invented because the government did not want its best and most innovative firms going out of business simply because they underestimated the difficulty of a particularly difficult *cutting-edge* project. However, the inventors of this type of contract did **not** intend it to be used for projects where *long-established conventional* technologies are being employed, such as the technologies being used on SLS or Ares-1.

Even more expense was added to the Constellation over-runs caused by cost-plus contracting because of the use of a set of Federal regulations known as *FAR* (see the glossary). This system of regulations allows NASA to "change the rules of the game" at any time during development without a renegotiating of the development contract. In effect they give NASA the ability to add or subtract features on a whim and to apply unnecessarily restrictive requirements that were not previously agreed upon and which may not necessarily improve safety or functionality. In vehicle development for the Commercial Crew program, problems with FAR are avoided via the use of *SAAs* (again see the glossary) which allow NASA *tremendous* oversight powers of such issues as safety, efficiency and cost, but without the financially crippling and time-wasting micro-control allowed under FAR rules.

Recall the development cost comparison shown earlier of the successful Falcon 9/Dragon flights to orbit versus Ares-1/Orion. The former was developed orders of magnitude more cheaply than what was spent on the latter. The contracting system used to pay SpaceX for Falcon 9/Dragon was a "pay for success only" type of contract. In other words, NASA laid out a series of goals for SpaceX to accomplish which would ultimately lead to a finished working system while meeting NASA's *very stringent* safety requirements. SpaceX only got a payment for any particular goal when they *successfully* completed that goal. ***No success, no pay***. Also, NASA did not pay all of the development costs associated with Falcon 9/Dragon, SpaceX had to pay the remainder. Furthermore, SAA was employed instead of FAR.

Obviously, there is a tremendous incentive for a company working under a "pay for success only" contract to produce a vehicle that performs **exactly** the way NASA wants it to perform and ***within budget***. Furthermore, ***the vehicle is more likely to be completed in a reasonable amount of time*** in order for the manufacturer to get paid by NASA as soon as possible. The lack of such incentives was a primary reason for the death of Ares-1, as it will be to the demise of SLS.

Why would a company be willing for NASA to pay *only part* of the development cost and not all of it? After all, how can a company hope to survive receiving less from NASA than what they put into it? In the case of SpaceX, the idea is that they can sell the Falcon 9 launcher to customers other than NASA. In fact, they already have a large backlog of orders from such customers. It's a win-win situation. NASA gets a new launch vehicle for far less than what they would normally pay and SpaceX now has a new product that they can market to recoup the unpaid portion of their development costs. Ultimately SpaceX should earn a profit from Falcon 9 for many years into the future.

However, the cost-plus contracting used for SLS is different in one way from that used for developing Ares-1 under project Constellation. To completely understand certain virtually insurmountable problems that SLS will encounter, it is instructive to know the financing difference between the two projects.

With Ares-1, unanticipated hardware changes (whether needed or not) that were not originally part of the design of the vehicle could be made and paid for, whether they functioned successfully or not. The same is true for SLS. However, in the case of Ares-1, the manufacturer could charge for both the work budgeted and any extra work done (that was not originally mentioned in the budget) and *not worry about what **amount** of money was actually budgeted for the year*. In order to pay the money owed for the unanticipated extra work, NASA needed to *add* money to Ares-1 development *over* what was originally budgeted. The only way this could be done was to take the needed extra money out of the budget from other NASA projects, thus allowing the cost of Ares-1 to balloon far above what was formally budgeted for it! Such extra unforeseen work included the earlier mentioned extra SRB segment, shock absorber, unanticipated alternate second-stage engine, etc. Though projects with unforeseen expensive problems were what cost-plus contracts were originally designed to handle, remember that the whole decision to go the Shuttle-derived route for Ares-1 was made under the assumption that development would get done quickly and cheaply **without** such major unforeseen **expensive** log jams because it was **assumed** the technology was so mature that it would require minimal changes!

Now in the case of SLS, there is a restriction that the total money being paid by NASA during any year cannot exceed what was budgeted for SLS for that year. This alternate type of cost-plus contract is sometimes referred to as "pay as you go". So if changes must be made, they can be made, but it means that other needed future NASA projects must be put off to a later date whenever SLS's development timeline is extended. The net result is that every time an unanticipated change occurs, the later the completion date of the first SLS rocket gets pushed into the future.

The above mentioned time adding circumstances are the pitfall that the Booz-Allen-Hamilton report warned of, and indeed, states that such extensive deadline push-backs will probably occur three to five years from the beginning of SLS development. (Booz-Allen-Hamilton 2011) Again, every extra year of development will also mean more added time delays, resulting in pushing SLS's inaugural flight further into the future.

What it all boils down to is this. It is impossible for SLS to go over its budget *for any particular year* as Ares-1 did. However, it will almost certainly go over what its initially figured *total* budget was stated to be, necessitating extension of its development *indefinitely*. Now the politicians probably don't mind this scenario with its theoretical perpetual job generation, but if our nation wants to actually have a *real* space program, it is truly bad news.

4.2 The "Whittle-knife Effect"

Cost-plus contracting is not the only problem with SLS that the Ares-1 project can shed some light on. Whenever politicians and upper level bureaucrats put together a gargantuan project such as SLS, they have a tendency to spread the work around to as many NASA research centers and traditional contractors as they possibly can. The idea is to make enough work to employ the **maximum** number of people **possible** and to avoid layoffs. Thus a large number of workers may be assigned to a project that would only need a few in the commercial world, or unnecessary extra features and byproducts may be produced in order to make the most jobs. After the points I made earlier regarding the motivations of the politicians who conceived it, how could SLS be otherwise? To see a more insightful and entertaining explanation of this principle, I suggest the reader look at an article written by space news journalist Mike Thomas. That article has led myself and others to refer to this process as the "The Whittle Knife Effect" in honor of Mr. Thomas' parable. (Thomas 2010)

Figure 12: Ares-1X on the launch pad (Image credit: NASA)

Again we turn to the development work on Ares-1 to instruct us. Perhaps the best (worst?) example ever perpetrated of a piece of "make-work" being spread around NASA centers was the so-called "*Ares-1X* " test that resulted in the only flight ever made during the Ares-1 project. Buzz Aldrin's explanation of this episode is so much better than anything I could come up with, so I'll just let him do the talking for me:

> *"Yes, the rocket that thundered aloft from NASA's Launch Pad 39B sure looked like an Ares-1. But that's where the resemblance stops. Turns out the solid booster was literally bought from the Space Shuttle program, since a five-segment booster being designed for Ares wasn't ready. So they put a fake can on top of the four-segmented motor to look like the real thing. Since the real Ares upper stage rocket engine, called the J-2X wasn't ready either, they mounted a fake upper stage. No Orion capsule was ready, so - you guessed it - they mounted a fake capsule with a real-looking but fake escape rocket that wouldn't have worked if the booster had failed. Since the guidance system for Ares wasn't ready either they went and bought a unit from the Atlas rocket program and used it instead. Oh yes, the parachutes to recover the booster were the real thing -- and one of the three failed, causing the booster to slam into the ocean too fast and banging the thing up."* (Aldrin b 2009)

The entire price of the launch was about $445 million (Block 2009) for a rocket that lofted a fake capsule to around 30 miles high and not anywhere close to reaching orbit using a common stock Space Shuttle SRB. For a perspective consider this, the altitude to which the fake dummy capsule reached was less than half of the altitude attained by Burt Rutan's privately-owned *manned* Spaceship One and about one quarter of the altitude of Alan Shepherd's first American manned spaceflight. Also the cost of that one 30 mile high flight was more than the ***total*** amount that NASA paid SpaceX for the first *three* flights *all the way to orbit* of Falcon 9 with two flights of the Dragon pressurized cargo spacecraft included.

In this instance, the ones to blame are some upper level agency officials at NASA who had some of their best aerospace engineers and technicians slap together this contraption from readily available parts without adequate preparation time. The 1X is often referred to as the "Frankenlauncher" because it was stitched together from various odds and ends, not unlike the construction of Mary Shelly's famous fictional monster.

Many suspect that a sense of urgency stemming from the anticipation of the imminent first test flight of SpaceX's Falcon 9 may have led to a hasty act of desperation: an attempt to demonstrate something would ***actually*** fly after billions had already been spent on Ares-1. Maybe, maybe not. Whether or not the cynics making this claim are correct, consider this: though it may not have been as much taxpayer money down the hole as some other boondoggles, it still doesn't change the fact that the so called "Ares-1X" was as much a real Ares-1 as an Estes model rocket is a spaceship. If those claiming a charade are indeed correct, let's hope a similar "demonstration" isn't dreamed up when schedule slips and budget overruns occur with increasing frequency on SLS.

There are more details to the SLS program that are just as screwy as Ares-1X. In order to satisfy the legal requirements (imposed by the politicians) that state that existing Shuttle hardware and contractors should be used as much as possible, more than one version of SLS is to be built.

The first version (called Block 1) would be capable of lifting 70 metric tons to low Earth orbit. It is to employ a modified version of ATK produced Shuttle SRBs, with the main modification being 5 engine segments to each SRB rather than 4 segments used on a standard Shuttle SRB. The 5 segment boosters were developed for Ares-1 after it was discovered that a 4 segment booster would not have adequate power to get the requisite amount of payload to orbit. Unlike the Shuttle SRBs, these boosters will not be reusable and are to be thrown away into the Atlantic Ocean after each flight. Two of these SRBs would be used, with one standing on either side of a central liquid fueled core booster powered by four Space Shuttle Main Engines (SSMEs). The payload would mount on top of the central liquid fueled booster. This vehicle was supposedly to be the one that would send NASA's Orion spacecraft on its first test flight. (NASA a 2012) However, it looks more and more as though this booster will not be completed before Orion is ready; thus, a decision has been made to have Orion's first flight in 2014 be on a Delta IV booster usually used to launch military satellites. (Leone 2012)

The politicians originally put pressure on NASA's administrator to use the 70 metric ton model of SLS as an "alternate" launch vehicle for sending crew to the ISS, in other words, as a "backup" in case problems delayed the Commercial Crew program. (Klingler a 2012) But it's a lousy idea even if both the first SLS and Orion could be completed before the independent commercial vehicles. Primarily, it is difficult to design launch vehicle/spacecraft systems that are dual-purpose space station taxi rides and deep space exploration vehicles. A vehicle designed for deep space would have numerous features and hardware unnecessary for the more mundane task of transport to ISS; thus, making transport to ISS vastly more costly. There are other reasons why this idea is a dumb one, but writing about them at this juncture would just delay continuing our discussion of what the plans are for the variants of SLS.

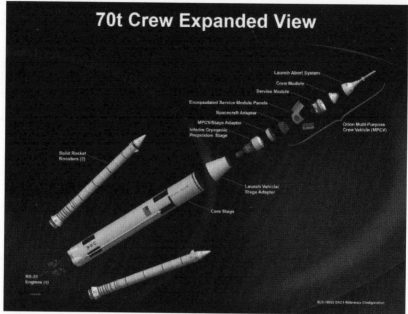

Figure 13: An expanded view of SLS Block 1 (Image credit: NASA)

The final Block 2 version of SLS would essentially be a Block 1 with a second stage above the central booster. The second stage would be powered by a new variant of the old Saturn V moon rocket's J-2 second stage engine. This model would be able to launch a gargantuan 130 tons to orbit.

By the way, before SLS was legislatively forced on the space agency, NASA asked both United Launch Alliance and SpaceX to submit quotes on the total cost of a heavy-lift vehicle with the same 130 metric tons to orbit payload as the final version of SLS. ULA said they could develop their version via various upgrades of their Atlas V launcher for a total of around $5.5 billion and *lift 10 tons more payload than SLS* to boot at 140 metric tons. (Barr & Kutter 2010) SpaceX's estimate included adding *an extra 20 metric tons of payload* (for a total mass to orbit of 150 metric tons) with a total cost of $2.5 billion. (Strickland a 2011) It looks like we could have *two* super heavy-lift launchers **more capable than SLS** for far less than the total spent on *just* SLS, even if SLS were to have no cost overruns!

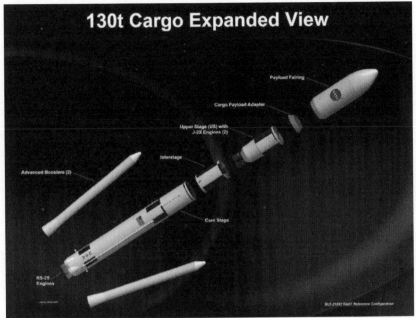

Figure 14: An expanded view of SLS Block 2 (Image credit: NASA)

If one takes at face value the contention of SLS supporters that a large super launcher of SLS's throw weight is required for deep space exploration, the fact that independently developed launchers of greater capability could be had for less brings up interesting legal implications. The existence of the above mentioned cost quotes of the ULA and SpaceX super launchers means that by requiring NASA to build SLS, Congress is tacitly violating the Commercial Space Act of 1998, because Title II, section 102, paragraph (a) *explicitly* states:

> *"(a) IN GENERAL.—Except as otherwise provided in this section, the Federal Government shall acquire space transportation services from United States commercial providers whenever such services are required in the course of its activities. To the maximum extent practicable, the Federal Government shall plan missions to accommodate the space transportation services capabilities of United States commercial providers."*

Rather than giving the reader just an external reference to this bill, the entire text of the bill is included after Chapter 9 of this book; however, it should be further noted that there is the alternative to SLS as proposed by Kraft and Moser and substantiated by the major studies mentioned earlier. This alternative would allow *even less* to be spent to do most of the operations of which SLS would be capable. The main NASA study describing this lower cost and safer advancement has been repressed (as has its supporters) deep within the bowels of the space agency, possibly because of the threat it represents to SLS.

As a result of this repression, it is possible that certain key mid-level and/or upper-level space agency officials have told the NASA Administrator little (if any) significant details about the study, or else the significance of its findings may have been purposely downplayed to him. Either way, there are two possible violations of the precepts of the Commercial Space Act of 1998: 1) the rejection of using ULA and/or SpaceX super HLVs mentioned earlier and 2) a dismissal of the alternative method using existing medium lift launchers in spite of NASA's own evidence of its greater effectiveness compared to SLS.

No matter what, the words of Space Frontier Foundation co-founder and former Reagan administration policy assistant *Jim Muncy* sum up the situation well:

> *"Everyone knows there is a train wreck on the horizon, and sooner or later it will become apparent we can't afford SLS. It's eating all the money we should be spending actually exploring."* (Berger 2012)

Concurring with Mr. Muncy, Peter A. Wilson who is both a professor at Georgetown University and an analyst for the legendary American think-tank known as the RAND Corporation, put forward the following summation of SLS:

> *"Simply put, the SLS program should be canceled now to free up approximately $10 billion programmed for this decade. This money could then be redirected to continue the planned flight tests of the Orion spacecraft with the much lower-cost Falcon Heavy booster while making a robust investment in a first-generation space station in the vicinity of the Moon. An investment in such a cislunar station would provide—by the early 2020s—a multifunctional platform to act as a fuel depot, a workstation for robotic operations on the Moon and a habitat to protect against the more intense radiation environment outside of the Earth's magnetic field. This station could even be used as a habitat during longer-duration human missions to an asteroid and eventually to Mars.*
> *Such a revised program would give NASA a real mid-2020s destination along with a rationale to help mobilize and sustain public, congressional and multilateral political and budgetary support during a period of federal fiscal austerity."* (Wilson 2013)

Mr. Wilson's words are very good advice with the problematic exception of his acceptance of Orion as an advantage. Unfortunately, because its faults are less obvious than SLS's, even some fairly knowledgeable people, such as he, think that way. A few of Orion-MPCV's drawbacks will be discussed in due course; however, because it is not *as much* of a capability crippler, it is not covered as extensively in this book as is SLS.

What it all boils down to is that we have the twin pitfalls of inappropriate cost-plus contracting *and* the Whittle Knife Effect going on with SLS. Of course, this dilemma is the same one that ultimately spelled doom for Ares-1. But the "monster rocket" as (Senator Nelson calls SLS) would not be the fastest method to get America exploring deep space quickly, even if NASA had a virtually unlimited budget and no other American entity could produce such a vehicle for less. The reason is that we would still have to wait a number of years while it is designed and built. As was pointed out earlier and as Kraft and Moser articulated, we *already have* launchers that can give us significant deep spacefaring capability **now**, but they are not being used for that purpose for two reasons: 1) because they are perceived as not offering as much pork to the interests of politicians from former shuttle related states and 2) the studies that support these alternately implemented human deep space missions (such as the type of missions proposed by Kraft and Moser) have been suppressed by certain powerful mid-level and upper-level factions within NASA itself who have a vested interest in keeping things going in the same way that they always have. Again, I do not expect the reader to blindly accept my word in this regard and I will present documented details backing these assertions in due course.

4.3 Negative effects of a finished and functioning SLS

Now everything discussed in this chapter so far refers only to the economic penalties from *just developing* SLS. It should be obvious by now that development is not likely to proceed to a point where a vehicle will be finished in the near future because of budget constraints coupled with unanticipated changes and the cost-plus contracting and FAR scheme being implemented. But for the sake of argument, let's say that a functioning SLS launch vehicle actually got produced. How useful would it be?

Actually employing SLS would harm NASA's budget as much or more as its development. One NASA estimate states a possible flight rate of only once per year! (Bergin a 2011) But let's be more optimistic about the flight rate and assume the often mentioned two flights a year and a cost of at least $1.5 billion per flight. (Strickland b 2011) The low flight rate would make it impractical for any real deep space exploration mission because such missions would need higher flight rates to loft the massive amounts of material needed, even when using a large launcher such as SLS. Worse, those two launches would require *at least* a $3 billion annual budget all by themselves.

Some SLS adherents pose a somewhat strange solution to the operational expense problem for SLS: use less launches of SLS in conjunction with already existing launch vehicles. *However, if you're going to use existing launch vehicles anyway, why use SLS at all?* After all, there are no necessary payloads the SLS can carry that can't be broken down into smaller (but still quite large) parts that are liftable by other less hefty rockets. To emphasize this point, now is a good time to scrutinize possible SLS launch costs as closely as we can without an as yet functioning vehicle to absolutely verify any conclusions we may surmise.

Some sources within the SLS program say that cost per launch would be about $500 million instead of more than $1.5 billion. Which estimate is more likely to be correct and why?

A good bit of the reason why the Space Shuttle was discontinued stemmed from its huge operational expenses. Expenses so massive that merely continuing to operate it would take money away from the development of the new Commercial Crew vehicles which were to replace it. Given this fact, it may be an instructive exercise to see how realistically estimated SLS launch costs would stack up again the cost of Shuttle launches.

Using a Shuttle per-launch cost of about $1.5 billion for comparison, some estimates state that even under the most optimistic of conditions the recurring per launch cost for SLS will be staggering. It would start around *at least* $1.3 billion for the initial 70 mt payload version and about $2.45 billion for the 130 mt model. (Strickland b 2011)

However, even those seemingly outrageous costs for SLS may be *extremely* optimistic when one considers that the baseline $1.5 billion dollar cost estimate for the Shuttle included the cost of *all* of the following: recurring manufacturing expense for each launch (remember it was not completely reusable), operation of the vehicle and the cost of the payload sent to orbit. By contrast, *the above cited figures for the two editions of SLS cover **only** the expense of manufacturing the final launch vehicle, and do **not** include operational costs and payload.* (Strickland b 2011) Also, remember that each SLS as originally proposed would be a totally throwaway vehicle, whilst much of the Shuttle's expensive hardware was recovered after each launch and recovery of that hardware helped to significantly lower its launch costs. (Strickland b 2011) To give the reader a further sense of proportion, consider a Falcon Heavy (capable of lofting three quarters of the payload of an SLS Block 1) would cost no more than $128 million in *total* launch vehicle price to the customer, but not including payload. (SpaceX a 2012) And the Falcon Heavy accomplishes this price while being a totally throwaway booster as well. However, as will be seen later, reusability of most or all of the Falcon Heavy is planned for the future which would further plummet the launch price.

Perhaps the clearest description of the "smoke and mirrors" method of determining launch vehicle cost used by SLS proponents was expressed by Clark Lindsey.

> *"Say the SLS program averages one to two flights per year. If the cost is $3B per in the years with one launch and $3.5B in the years with two launches then NASA will claim that a SLS flight costs $500M (i.e. the marginal cost, which is the cost to produce one more unit output). This is obviously ridiculous. The meaningful cost is $6.5B/3 = $2.17B per flight. For low production numbers, it is only the average cost that is significant, not marginal cost. (Usually NASA just guesses how much one more flight would cost but I used this year to year comparison to make the marginal cost more explicit.)"* (Lindsey c 2013)

At this point I would like to make a side note. After a "competition" was proposed for the boosters on a Block 1B version and Block 2 version of SLS, ATK has proposed altering their 5 segment SRB to be reusable in a similar manner to the way SRB's were reused for the Shuttle. They call this altered booster a RSRM. (Bergin a 2011) The first flights of SLS would be flown as the Block 1A model with the originally offered throwaway SRB.

Reusability may be a competitive advantage for ATK when competing against Teledyne Brown Engineering and Aerojet, but it probably will *not* result in *as much* cost savings for SLS as it did for Shuttle. This situation is due to the fact that the Shuttle had *two types* of reusable hardware: the SRBs *and* the spacecraft (i.e., the Shuttle Orbiter). Assuming the ATK booster is chosen, only the SRB would be reusable (remember Orion-MPCV would be throwaway).

No matter which booster is chosen, an operational SLS would still be an expensive boondoggle because: 1) the relatively small amount of reusability added by ATK's new SRB probably would not have a hugely significant impact, 2) the use of FAR and cost-plus contracting, 3) the "Whittle Knife Effect" and 4) even if such a huge payload booster was *required*, there are more viable sources available from ULA and SpaceX for less cost that would also not be subject to the *perpetual* wait for a finished booster as would be the case for a finished Block 2 SLS.

Remember, even if a completed SLS was ready to be launched, *there would be no payloads available for it of the size it was designed to lift.* The most it would be able to do would be to lift multiple smaller payloads in one launch. Payloads that could instead be put up with multiple medium sized one-payload-per-launch vehicles, *but SLS would do so at much greater total launch cost.*

Earlier it was mentioned that NASA should be doing truly pioneering cutting-edge exploration missions and in the process of doing such exploration, serve as a technology incubator for the commercial space industry. As will be revealed, in order to do that frontier exploration *NASA will eventually need some much* **more advanced** *space vehicles of a type that have* **never** *been built before.* NASA should be working on designing, developing, building and testing those exciting *new types* of vehicles with modern technologies rather than "reinventing the wheel" with their own large heavy-lift launch vehicle derived from old technology Shuttle-era hardware. If huge *conventional* launch vehicles of such gargantuan power as SLS are ever *truly* needed, then industry already has the technologies, experience and manufacturing base needed to make them far more economically and efficiently than via a project centrally overseen and minutely controlled by NASA. There isn't a better way of closing this chapter than to give the reader a real-world example proving this point.

Recall the fact that the Block 1 version of SLS is supposed to have a maximum payload to LEO of 70 metric tons and would come to pass as the result of billions of American taxpayer dollars spent. Now think about the fact the SpaceX is simultaneously developing its *Falcon Heavy* (SpaceX a 2012) HLV with a payload capacity of 53 metric tons; that is, 75% of the payload capacity of SLS Block 1 and is expected to be ready for launch *years earlier* than the Block 1. Also consider this fact: *SpaceX is building this rocket without one dime of taxpayer money because they are footing the entire development cost themselves!* When Falcon Heavy is finished, it will be the most powerful rocket since the Saturn V moon rocket, but will have been financed *only* via private means with *no* government financial contributions. Meanwhile, even the Block 1 version of SLS would still be years away from its *originally* predicted 2017 finish date, whilst the estimate of that finish date will probably continually slip later beyond 2017.

But let's be realistic, SpaceX *could* run into unexpected technical problems during the development of Falcon Heavy. However, the design of Falcon Heavy is technically sound, consisting primarily of three Falcon 9 cores strapped together. Given that fact, there is no reason why it won't be finished, no matter what unanticipated problems are encountered. It would be hard to imagine any major glitch that would take them more than a year or two to fix. This *pessimistic* scenario would still allow them to finish it around the most optimistic 2017 launch date of SLS Block 1 and possibly a bit before. However, as was already mentioned, Block 1 will probably not be ready by that date.

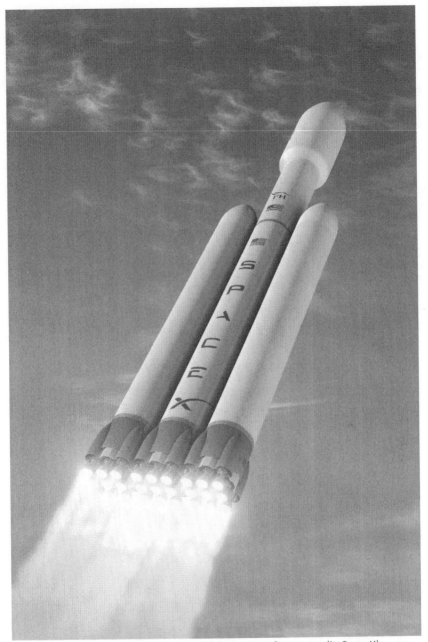

Figure 15: Artist's conception of Falcon Heavy (Image credit: SpaceX)

Now ponder this idea. *If SpaceX can build a rocket with three quarters of the payload capacity of the SLS Block 1* **without** *taxpayer money, what could they do with* **just a fraction** *of the money that is being spent on SLS?*

Putting it bluntly, developing a *conventional* technology launch vehicle of *any kind* is now a relatively routine industrial endeavor, far beneath the *state-of-the-art* projects that NASA *could* be working on. So much so that it is virtually *an insult* of the agency to have it develop SLS, because it is an *unnecessary waste* of its resources and exceptional talent that could instead be expanding our spaceflight capabilities far beyond where they are now. The next chapter will amply illustrate this point.

Chapter 5: A practical, affordable and *ambitious* national space program *starting now*

"Reach low orbit and you're halfway to anywhere."
-- Robert Heinlein

Even if SLS could be completed within the time frame its proponents claim it can, we would still be waiting years for it to be finished. Meanwhile we would remain stuck in *Low Earth Orbit* (commonly referred to as *LEO*) where we have been spinning our metaphorical wheels for the last several decades. But it just so happens that we don't have to wait all those years to actually begin our outward spiral into the Solar System and we don't have to increase NASA's budget to do it. It turns out that *practically all of the marvelous deep space missions being touted for SLS can be accomplished cheaper, easier, safer, sooner and more reliably with* **already existing** *launch vehicles*.

5.1 A truly innovative proposal from ULA

The earlier mentioned Kraft/Moser article touched on some of these alternatively executed missions and stated they offered both substantial cost reductions and job creation, but did not give detailed estimates of cost savings. In contrast, recall the NASA, industry and university studies cited earlier. The earliest initial groundbreaking study of those three was ULA's *A Commercially Based Lunar Architecture* (Zegler, Kutter & Barr 2009). It **compared** estimated costs for doing deep space missions using a shuttle-derived heavy lift vehicle (such as SLS) to the use of rockets in the existing commercial market in conjunction with propellant depots.

The study from 2009 was released *before* project Constellation was cancelled and both Ares-1 and Ares-V were still living works in progress. Remember, SLS is essentially a resurrected Ares-V, so if you substitute SLS for Ares-V everywhere the Ares-V appears in the study, you essentially have a report in which the underlying principles very much apply today. Another remarkable aspect of the study was the ULA engineers' realistic view that this innovative architecture could not be successful unless other commercial space companies (such as SpaceX) were also involved in its execution.

Perhaps there is no more eloquent refutation of the "humongous Shuttle-derived rocket fallacy" than is mentioned on page 4 of the ULA study:

> *"It is easy to be dazzled by the drama of astronauts lifting off on a pillar of flame but most of the work of going to the moon is just about moving propellants. At least 70% of the job of launching mass to LEO, the first step on the way to the moon, is moving the liquid hydrogen and oxygen we will need for the subsequent steps. Because of its magnitude, moving propellant is far and away the most important element of any lunar architecture but it is often wholly ignored. It is crucial that the handling and moving of propellants be very efficient. The more efficiently propellants are delivered for all the various purposes the greater the overall system affordability and performance. To a lesser extent this is also true of cargo - the tools and consumables needed for lunar operations."* (Zegler, Kutter & Barr 2009)

The same study makes the point that by not going the Shuttle-derived HLV route there is *more than enough money left over* to develop a lunar lander, called *Altair*, which can also be derived from existing launch vehicle hardware. Altair could ferry up to four people to and from the lunar surface as well as cargo such as large land roving vehicles.

Of course, the above excerpt makes specific reference to expeditions to the Moon, but as was pointed out earlier, the same principle holds for all missions beyond LEO, be they a trip to a NEO, Mars, etc. Stating the issue more succinctly, just getting to LEO is currently a major fraction of the cost in *any* of those scenarios and the lack of in-space propellant depots increases the cost of operations above LEO even further. Indeed, on page 1 of the same study, this very point is made:

> *"This architecture encourages the exploration of the moon to be conducted not in single, disconnected missions, but in a continuous process which builds orbital and surface resources year by year. The architecture and vehicles themselves are directly applicable to Near Earth Object and Mars exploration and the establishment of a functioning depot at earth-moon L2 provides a gateway for future high-mass spacecraft venturing to the rest of the solar system."*

This alternative method to SLS has the further advantage of allowing significant human-crewed exploratory missions beyond LEO *without* increases to NASA's budget, as will be indicated with further third party evidence in later chapters. Furthermore, this situation permits ambitious unmanned robotic missions to occur more frequently because *less expensive* human spaceflight will be less likely to rob such automated missions of the funds they need (as would be the case if SLS continues).

5.2 The suppression of NASA's ground-breaking propellant depot report

Recall the study mentioned previously called *Propellant Depot Requirements Status Report* (HSF 2011). A cost breakdown of all phases and technologies required for an exploratory mission to a Near Earth Asteroid (or NEA) are laid out in detail by comparing two different plans: one plan using an SLS-type Shuttle-derived HLV versus another which would use the SpaceX Falcon Heavy launcher. As shown on page 16 of the report, it would take 18 years on the former plan to ultimately culminate with an actual crewed mission to an asteroid at a total cost of $143 billion dollars over the entire time period; that is, about $7.9 billion per year and a huge chunk of NASA's yearly budget. A goodly fraction of the overall cost and lead time is development of the Shuttle-derived heavy lift vehicle (such as SLS). Now contrast that to the scenario using the Falcon Heavy on page 15 of the report, whose cost breakdown comes to a total of $64 billion over the same amount of time for an annual budget of only $3.6 billion per year. The latter figure is less than half the cost of the other course and a relatively minor fraction of the agency's annual budget.

The first clue of an active faction in NASA's upper level management attempting to suppress all discussion of better alternatives to SLS was revealed by Congressional Representative Dana Rohrabacher. He is currently the vice-chairman of the House Science, Space, and Technology Committee and perhaps the foremost Congressional critic of SLS. In Mr. Rohrabacher words:

> *"When NASA proposed on-orbit fuel depots in this Administration's original plan for human space exploration, they said this game-changing technology could make the difference between exploring space and falling short. Then the depots dropped out of the conversation, and NASA has yet to provide any supporting documents explaining the change."* (Cowing b 2011)

About a month later, the results of the internal NASA study (which SLS supporters had fervently tried to prevent seeing the light of day) were leaked out in an act of defiance by agency engineers involved in the study. Both the attempted suppression of the anti-SLS faction and the existence of the report were brought to light by renowned space policy journalist Keith Cowing. In Mr. Cowing's words:

"Right now there is a slow-motion purge underway within OCT and across the agency to move anyone who thinks beyond the SLS mindset in ways that could do things in a much less costly fashion with much greater flexibility." (Cowing b 2011)

As for the contents of the study, here again is Mr. Cowing (I've boldfaced one part of the quote for emphasis):

"This presentation "Propellant Depot Requirements Study - Status Report - HAT Technical Interchange Meeting - July 21, 2011" is a distilled version of a study buried deep inside of NASA. The study compared and contrasted an SLS/SEP architecture with one based on propellant depots for human lunar and asteroid missions. **Not only was the fuel depot mission architecture shown to be less expensive, fitting within expected budgets, it also gets humans beyond low Earth orbit a decade before the SLS architecture could.***"* (Cowing b 2011)

So the study called *Propellant Depot Requirements Status Report* (HSF 2011) puts forward a direct comparison of the costs, capabilities, etc of SLS (or *SDV HLLV*, as it is referred to in the report) versus alternative methods of doing space missions to the Moon, a NEO and Mars. It indicates depot-based methods using *existing* commercial launch vehicles would save *many billions of dollars* over using SLS and make ambitious missions much easier to actually accomplish within the fluctuating budgets that Congress is fond of imposing on NASA. Furthermore, this alternate direction would allow such missions to be done *much sooner* than otherwise would be possible going the more expensive SLS route (under the *extremely* optimistic assumption that SLS gets finished at all).

5.3 The initial Georgia Tech and NASA reports

The above mentioned NASA study came to light a few months after the release of another study which refuted the necessity of an SLS class vehicle for ambitious space missions. In this case it was a joint effort of Georgia Tech and The National Institute of Aerospace called *Near Term Space Exploration with Commercial Launch Vehicles Plus Propellant Depots* under the leadership of Langley Distinguished Professor and co-Director of the Georgia Tech Center for Aerospace Systems Engineering, Allan Wilhite. (Wilhite a et al. 2010) Here I paraphrase the principal conclusions of the report for greater clarity for the lay person:

1) Propellant depots, large spacecraft for exploring deep space, and other large structures needed for pioneering deep space missions can be accomplished by assembling them piece-meal in space using already existing medium lift launch vehicles to get them to their assembly location in space.

2) A good bit of the savings comes from the fact that 80% to 90% of the mass that needs to be lifted is propellant. Such a payload is easily divided across multiple launches of medium lift commercial vehicles.

3) This alternative method saves the enormous development costs associated with an SLS style launcher.

4) The combination of *extremely low flight rates* and *high costs unique to large Shuttle-derived HLVs* (such as SLS) is eliminated. *Furthermore, the use of previously existing launchers decreases the total expense by spreading the over-all cost via more flights and more customers (other than NASA) that use those launch vehicles.* After all, these are the same launchers that put up satellites used for communications, GPS, weather forecasting, military reconnaissance, etc.

One of the favorite tactics of SLS supporters is the assertion that using medium lift launchers for deep space missions is a precarious route since the increased flight rate means a higher chance of a launch vehicle failure and it is further assumed even just one failed launch would be a major setback. The earlier mentioned NASA study (HSF 2011) puts forth evidence that this argument is a red herring. Remember, each launcher would entail a very small fraction of the cost of an SLS vehicle and could be replaced very quickly after an accident because it is readily available for purchase on the commercial market off of a standard production line. Also, most of the launch payloads would be merely large amounts of cheap propellant to fill a depot instead of a spacecraft worth billions of dollars; therefore, again not a deal breaker.

Another criticism of the use of medium sized launch vehicles is the claim that the companies which produce them would not be able to keep up with the increased demand for their vehicles. The earlier mentioned NASA study (HSF 2011) makes three points in this regard. First, the launch rate, though higher than previously experienced, would still not be excessively brisk. Second, the launch vehicle production facilities are *currently underutilized* and the operation will merely use capacity which is currently wasted. Third, having multiple vehicle providers should insure that one manufacturer can make up for any slack of production by another.

So the burying of the NASA study results showing the relative cost and efficacy comparison of SLS to the depot and medium lift launcher alternative (along with the ignoring of the ULA and Wilhite et al. studies) constitute yet another disregard of the spirit of the Commercial Space Act of 1998 beyond the ignoring of HLV proposals from ULA and SpaceX.

5.4 Evidence of incorrect assumptions by ASAP

When it comes to SLS and Orion versus commercial launch vehicles and spacecraft, one of the main culprits within NASA guilty of major hypocrisy is the *Aerospace Safety Advisory Panel* or *ASAP*. This panel proposed that all participants in the Commercial Crew program perform *multiple unmanned* flights of their launch vehicles and spacecraft before humans are allowed to fly in them. There's absolutely nothing wrong with that position. In fact, it is how it *should* be for *any* new launch vehicle and/or spacecraft. Why? Because any competent aerospace engineer will tell you, **the only way to get a realistic idea of the safety of any flying system is to have an actual flight history long enough to obtain reliable data.** For any particular vehicle, only *multiple* test flights give you the necessary length of time needed to collect a high enough volume of data and flight experience for adequately evaluating how safe a system is. However, even then, there are always unanticipated problems that will eventually result in fatality, cases in point from the Space Shuttle program: the O-ring incident with *Challenger* and the ice fragment impact with *Columbia*.

Ever heard of a *totally* crash-proof airplane? Even with extensive test flights and computer simulations, the best that competent engineers can do is to minimize the chance of fatalities as much as possible with *both* computer simulations *and* multiple actual flights. But you can bet that if you do not have *numerous actual* test flights before passengers fly, there *certainly* will eventually be fatal situations in the real world *which weren't accounted for in the simulations* that could have been prevented by detecting them operationally during test flights. Even with the test flights, all such situations will not be detected, but at least the probability of catastrophe is significantly lessened. This situation exists because *the best* of engineers (despite their impressive knowledge and skills) are fallible humans and *nobody* can possibly think of *all* the things that can *potentially* go wrong in actual flight. So putting any *experimental* aircraft or spacecraft into its continuous routine passenger service without an adequate history of test flights (regardless of the number of simulations run or how advanced those simulations are) is the height of foolishness.

Where the hypocrisy comes into play is ASAP's stance on SLS. They claim that, after all of NASA's computer simulations are run, there will need to be *only* one test flight of SLS before crew actually flies with it. (Bergin b 2012) Their validation of this strategy is *their claim* that NASA has more experience with successfully *developing* human spaceflight systems than the companies developing the Commercial Crew vehicles. They further state that commercial companies are more likely to cut corners on safety even though evidence will be supplied herein which shows at least one commercial launch vehicle company has decided *on its own* to follow *tougher* safety precautions beyond what NASA requires on its own systems!

Proponents of the "one flight is test enough" position point out that the Saturn V had only one unmanned test flight before human crew flew on it and the Space Shuttle carried crew on its very first flight. It is conceivable that this was at least a fairly rational option back then because the people who developed Saturn V had previously designed and developed *successful* hardware to put people in orbit with the Mercury and Gemini programs. There were a lot of Apollo people with their successful design and development experience with <u>Saturn 1B</u> and Saturn V who were behind the genesis of the Shuttle. It should also be noted that during those days, NASA was not as adverse to risk taking as it is now.

But remember what I told you in earlier. *Nobody* now at NASA and its traditional contractors has *designed and developed* a spacecraft that has *actually* sent humans to orbit since the Shuttle was developed several decades ago. They haven't even been successful at finishing operational unmanned suborbital test vehicles built as test models for bigger manned orbital launch vehicles. Two such failed examples include: the <u>X-33</u> Venture Star and <u>X-34</u> projects of the late 1990s and early 2000s (this lack of success happened more because of the way NASA and its contractors were required to go about doing the projects, than a lack of technical expertise). Further recall that many of the engineering professionals at the Commercial Crew companies were formerly some of the *best* that NASA and its traditional contractors had. They received the same training and have similar work experience as their NASA counterparts. So the people *currently* at NASA now have no more knowledge, expertise or experience when it comes to *designing and developing* passenger vehicles that have *actually* put people in orbit than their Commercial Crew program counterparts. Thus, SLS and Orion would have *neither* more *nor* less likelihood of being safe than Commercial Crew launch vehicles in situations where *neither* has demonstrated previous flight heritage.

However, the Commercial Crew launch vehicles *do* have significant orbital flight *heritage* because of Commercial Cargo launches and the competitive private launch market, and so at this stage they are more likely to be safer than SLS! *Given this fact, to make sure SLS is **reasonably** safe to the same level as commercial launch vehicles would require unmanned multiple launches of that vehicle, just as it does for vehicles used under the Commercial Crew program.* In other words, the members of ASAP accept both the <u>second myth</u> and <u>fifth myth</u> mentioned in Chapter 2 as unquestionable facts when there is no rational foundation to do so.

In lieu of multiple test flights, ASAP claim NASA can do a *Loss of Crew* estimate or *LOC* that will insure a reasonable amount of safety using data from computer simulations and the one test flight. (Bergin b 2012) But a truly accurate LOC without extensive real flight data is indeed a *fantasy* worthy of being called a White Queen thought process.

Though their excuse for this drastically abbreviated test period for SLS is their unrealistic claim of *purported* greater experience of NASA personnel, according to some outside experts that is not the *real* reason. As expressed by columnist Clark Lindsey of the online space industry journal *New Space Watch* and the space-related topics website known as *Space for All at HobbySpace*:

> *"The ASAP is concerned that commercial firms will cut corners to save money and undermine the safety of their vehicles. On the other hand, ASAP implicitly accepts that NASA cannot afford to do multiple test flights of the SLS so it allows the agency to cut a huge corner and fly a crew on an extremely complex vehicle after insufficient test flights, justifying this with the science fiction of the LOC estimate"* (Lindsey a 2012)

It boils down to this: *in reality the members of ASAP know that SLS is so expensive that NASA **can't afford** to do more than one or two test flights.* This type of economically induced recklessness is yet another reason to axe the SLS program.   OK, maybe they'll get lucky and not have a failure on multiple human crewed flights. But that doesn't change the fact that if they think it is reckless for the Commercial Crew participants to fly people without multiple flights, then *it has to be* just as reckless for NASA to be doing so with SLS. Again, this is true **because 1) the current personnel at NASA have no more experience** designing **and developing a passenger vehicle that has** actually **flown to orbit than the Commercial Crew people do and 2) there will not be enough flight data for a high level of confidence in the LOC and hence the safety of SLS.**

So there is *no safety advantage* of using SLS instead of existing commercial boosters for any space operation and possibly a *safety disadvantage* due to insufficient testing before humans ride it. In fact, as stated in a presentation by Professor Wilhite related to the Georgia Tech comparative studies:

> *"With the heritage of commercial launch successes and redundant mixed fleet vehicles, probability for a launch success of an asteroid mission is projected to be substantially safer than a new HLLV (92% versus 58%). "* (Wilhite c 2013)

Of course in the above quote, one can read "SLS" in place of the phrase "a new HLLV".

But as we will see in a later chapter, ASAP's near unquestioning belief in the second and fifth myths and an *assumed* superiority of cost-plus contracting and FAR is so great that they would like to see an end to the SAA agreements that are fostering the impressive progress being made by the Commercial Crew program -- as expressed on page 5 of ASAP's 2012 report. (Dyer a et al. 2013) Thus, one of the greatest dangers of seriously stifling the budding commercial spaceflight industry comes from the possibility that those particular ASAP recommendations could be taken seriously.

5.5 The need for in-space infrastructure

Let's look at specific *infrastructure* projects that need to be implemented *in space* for both deep space exploration missions as well as economic space exploitation ventures. This is infrastructure we can begin building starting *now* rather than waiting year after year for the completion of SLS with its associated waste of tens of billions of dollars.

After obtaining lower cost flight from Earth to LEO, the biggest source of cost savings for exploratory and exploitive missions to the Moon, asteroids and Mars would be derived from essential in-space infrastructure. ***Space flight cannot become a thriving economic powerhouse and extensive job creating force until the necessary support facilities are built in space that will allow it to do so.*** Throughout history it has been the case that no form of long distance transportation became convenient until the supporting infrastructure was built, and spaceflight is no exception. Before talking about in-space infrastructure, it may be instructive to look at how the infrastructure in other earlier transportation industries came about and government's role in the development of those industries.

In the case of long distance locomotive travel, an extensive network of railways, depots, and maintenance rail yards was created. For extended journeys via automobile, what was needed was an enormous network of high quality roads and bridges. Practical world-wide air transportation would be impossible without the numerous airports, mechanical service facilities and navigational aids implemented for that purpose. In every single one of those circumstances, government had a role in providing at least part of the infrastructure that allowed commercial entities to turn each transportation technology into a profitable industry. But government also provided kick-start financial incentives to allow those industries to reach their economy stimulating potential.

In the case of railroads, the federal government granted rights of way to the rail companies and also the use of any resources (such as timber for railroad ties) from lands encountered along the way. Local municipal, county and state governments would often have bond issues to pay for construction of actual local railroads linking cities with an eye toward increasing commerce.

Of course, the federal government was the primary instigator of the elaborate web of extensive quality paved roads spanning the nation, the climax being the interstate highway system of freeways. The local state, county and municipal governments built the roads to get people and goods easily between cities within an area and to allow access to the main interstate system. The creation of this infrastructure would not have been profitable for the automotive industry itself to undertake. Without this government investment, automobile travel would have remained restricted to local jaunts close to home as it was in the early twentieth century.

For air transportation, it was typically local governments that financed airports, but by itself this would not have been enough to bring about a thriving aviation industry. What further kick-started commercial aviation was the federal government's contracting for transportation of air mail before passenger flight caught on in a big way. Once airplane fleet companies were guaranteed to make money from hauling mail, they decided to try making some extra money by encouraging passengers to travel along with the mail. They then quickly realized they could make money from primarily transporting passengers to destinations faster than rail or car, and the airline industry was born. America was the only country to tackle the problem in this way with the result that American aviation came to dominate the world, leading to an international aviation industry in which English became the standard language of air communication and (for good or ill) altitude measured in feet rather than meters and air distances in miles instead of kilometers.

In all of the above instances, a dynamic new transportation industry was started, not by the government designing and developing its own locomotives, cars, trucks or airplanes to the exclusion of other vehicle sources, but by the government supplying necessary *infrastructure* and *financial incentives* to help get the industry to a point where it was self-sustaining.

Now that we have covered the precedents for infrastructure development and the traditional role of American government therein, we are finally at a juncture where it makes sense to discuss the infrastructure needed for truly practical deep space transportation and what strategy will maximize the effectiveness of government participation in helping create a thriving industry that will greatly stimulate the national economy.

The deep space infrastructure component that is perhaps getting the most attention from NASA lately is something called a *gateway*. It is another innovative concept that Buzz Aldrin has pushed for many years. NASA would like their gateway to be located at a place in space called *Lagrangian point[3] 2* or *L2* where it would act as a way-station for human exploration trips to the Moon or deeper into interplanetary space. (Matthews b 2012) One of its key features would be a depot for supplying spacecraft with the propellant they need to continue on to much farther destinations. It may also serve as a point where astronauts can transfer between spacecraft capable of taking off/landing on Earth and spacecraft more suitable for deep space travel.

Figure 16: A proposed inflatable gateway (Image credit: NASA)

---

[3] The Earth-Moon Lagrangian points are 5 different places in deep space where the gravitational pull of the Earth and Moon cancel each other, so that any object placed there essentially stays put relative to the Earth and Moon. Some very modest rocket thrust is *occasionally* required to maintain position, but that extremely infrequent station-keeping burn consumes very little propellant. This characteristic makes these places prime candidates for gateway locations. L2 (also known as EML-2) is located above the far side of the Moon at a distance of about 277,000 miles from Earth. For a more extensive explanation, see *Lagrangian points* in this book's glossary.

5.6 Attempted hijacking of the in-space infrastructure issue

Lately there has been talk of using SLS to launch the largest components of the gateway, no doubt partly as justification for the existence of that launcher. However, reliance on SLS would doom the gateway to excessive cost overruns and ultimate failure due to all of the previously discussed economic shortcomings of that vehicle. In the words of space pundit Charles Lurio of the professional space industry publication called *The Lurio Report*:

> *"NASA is trying to find uses for a rocket that Congress forced the agency and the White House to accept. You can do this mission much more cheaply using rockets such as Falcon Heavy, Falcon 9, Atlas and fuel depots. Mega rockets like the SLS are for showing off, not for serious space exploration"* (Boyle 2012)

As mentioned in an earlier chapter, there exists a follow up study to the previously mentioned Georgia Tech paper that does a *direct comparison* of implementing a gateway with existing commercial launch vehicles versus SLS Block 1 and/or SLS Block 2; that is, assuming SLS could ever become an actual functional launch vehicle (which is a very doubtful assumption for reasons outlined previously). The study compares such issues as safety, ease of implementation, and cost of using each method. Here are some of its key conclusions:

> *"Commercial launch with propellant depot architectures significantly improves the extensibility and mission payload capability by providing a robust framework for all foreseen missions in the next 30 years. Adding to commercial launches every few months provides experienced and focused workforce to improve safety, operational learning for reduced costs and higher launch reliability, reduce launch costs depending on the government/industry business model.*
>
> *The depot framework allows multiple competitors for propellant delivery that is low-risk, hands-off way for international partners to contribute because it is not in the critical "mission" path and provides redundant alternatives available if critical launch failure occurs. The architecture provides reduced critical path mission complexity (Automated Rendezvous and Docking events, number of unique elements), provides additional mission flexibility by variable propellant load.*
>
> *Commonality with COTS/commercial/DoD vehicles will allow sharing of fixed costs between programs and "right-sized" vehicle for ISS, thus stimulate US and international commercial launch industry. Development risk is reduced by eliminating four space elements including: the major Earth-to-orbit launch vehicle and solar electric propulsion transfer vehicle, large mass margins with*

current and proposed launch systems, and the Cryogenic Propellant Storage and Transfer in-space technology demonstration program." (Wilhite b et al. 2012)

Translating the above quoted paragraphs for the lay reader, they boil down to these main points:

1) For a period of around the next 30 years, the proposed alternative architecture will allow us to not only penetrate deeper into space than SLS would allow, but also permit larger and more ambitious missions within a NASA budget that isn't likely to be expanded and could even see some budget reduction.

2) The large standing army of employees needed to prepare and support SLS along with its ridiculously low flight rate contribute to extremely high operational costs on, not only a per launch basis, but also a per pound to orbit basis when compared to the alternative architecture. In contrast, the commercial launcher/depot architecture would result in more operationally experienced support personnel whose more constant and continual flight experience permits them to respond more competently and rapidly when needed; thereby, resulting in faster acquisition of critical skills and the associated rapid ramping up to increased levels of flight safety and much higher launch reliability.

3) The increased economies of scale stemming from the much higher flight rate will help to significantly bring down both manufacturing and operational costs of the commercial launch vehicles used.

4) This alternative method more easily integrates multiple vehicle suppliers into the mix, with competition among companies potentially providing even more cost reduction and lessening the number of possible critical failure points by way of having multiple *different* launch vehicles. For instance, ULA, *Orbital Sciences*, and SpaceX could all offer launch vehicles for sending propellant to the needed depots, but if one company's launch vehicle experiences a serious operational problem, the other companies can pick up the slack with their launchers. What's more, having multiple vehicles of different makes gives international partners a chance to significantly participate (such as the European Ariane launcher and the Russian Soyuz), offering even more redundant backup and sharing of project costs.

5) The fact that the American commercial launch vehicles are also used for Defense Department missions and commercial satellites will raise flight rates even further, thereby offering still more increased economies of scale leading to even lower launch costs.

6) Because of the extensive use of *already existing* operational launchers with an extensive flight history, the enormous development expense entailed with SLS can be eliminated along with much of the cost of developing its supporting flight operational infrastructure.

7) The increased use of existing commercial launchers will greatly *stimulate* both the US and international commercial launch industry, leading to a corresponding increase in jobs in these industries.

Unfortunately, all of the above facts will not prevent proponents of SLS from trying to use the need of a gateway for deep space operations as an excuse to continue development of SLS, whilst simultaneously ignoring how other launch vehicles could be used to implement such a gateway sooner, safer and cheaper.

Furthermore, people pushing the idea of using SLS for gateway operations (by having it haul modules for the construction of the gateway and subsequently supply propellant and transport passengers to and from the gateway) would saddle the project with a very cost inefficient construction plan. Specifically, I refer to their proposal to use leftover modules from the construction of ISS as well as the construction of new modules of this type. ISS style modules have a lot of bulk by volume and are fairly heavy, thus requiring a big heavy lift vehicle of the SLS's size. Of course, this is just another attempt to come up with a justification for SLS and give its proponents an excuse to say it has a rational purpose; thereby, insuring the continued flow of billions of dollars coming to their favorite earmark. As always, they are trying to take a vehicle they want, which has no purpose, and force a purpose to fit it. It is in this way that they hope to silence critics who call SLS "The Rocket to Nowhere".

There is another significant disadvantage with construction of the gateway using the traditional space station hardware approach that is being proposed by SLS pushers. Better space station modules have been developed by *Bigelow Aerospace* in the years since the International Space Station was built. Because these *much lighter modules* can be launched in a collapsed/folded-up form and inflated into their final large volume, they can be flown on more modest rockets than SLS and can have an even greater habitable volume after they are inflated than the ISS style modules.

As will be discussed, they also offer better protection against meteoroids and unhealthy radiation.

Many people have never heard of Bigelow Aerospace, but this company has actually had a couple of test space station modules in orbit for years. (Bigelow 2012) Additionally, NASA has recently signed a $17.8 million contract with Bigelow to produce a spacious doughnut-shaped additional module for the ISS called *BEAM* (or *Bigelow Expandable Activity Module*) which would add a significant amount of living space and storage space to the station. (Lindsey b 2013) The highly unusual shape of this module compared to existing space station modules offers the possibility of some unique applications that will eventually be covered.

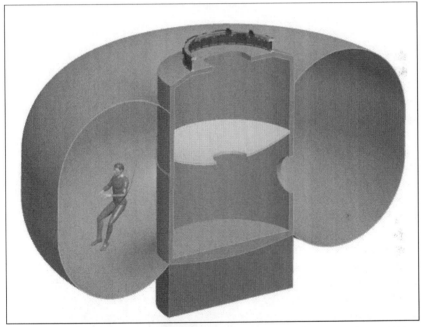

Figure 17: Cut-away showing interior of the Bigelow BEAM (Image credit: NASA)

This module could be exactly the kind of large building block NASA needs to construct a practical functioning deep space gateway. It's Vectran® based walls offer greater protection from micro-meteoroid impacts than the aluminum walls of traditional ISS modules. Also, when primary cosmic radiation strikes the outer walls of an aluminum ISS module, it can cause secondary radiation to be dispersed within the module, striking the vulnerable living bodies of astronauts inside. The alternate construction of BEAM eliminates much of that harmful radiation. (Marks 2013)

SLS proponents argue their gateway proposal would make use of a large habitation module made for ISS that has been stored away for years at the Marshall Space Flight center in Alabama. (Money b 2012) But any savings from using such already existing equipment will be more than offset by both the huge development costs and enormous launch costs for SLS. However, even that disadvantage is irrelevant if the scenario of exhaustion of the SLS budget occurs with years more of uncompleted development needed, as was indicated as likely by the Booz-Allen-Hamilton report. (Booz-Allen-Hamilton 2011) The words of space issues pundit Stewart Money summarize the situation well:

> *"Moving into the era of commercial re-supply for the station we already have, ISS; this [the gateway project] is a proposal which could benefit from the lessons of COTS and incorporate the role of similar partnerships in lowering costs and achieving viability (SpaceX, Bigelow), or it could follow an all too familiar path of top down design with pre-determined infrastructure (SLS, Orion) and absorb another decade of high costs and limited progress. In any event, it will be interesting to track the progress of this proposal and how it fares versus any alternatives, or as many fear, nothing at all."* (Money b 2012)

5.7 Other needed technologies that SLS inhibits

But launch vehicles and spacecraft for traveling between Earth and L2 are not the only things we need for deep space utilization and exploration.

As I will discuss in Chapter 9, another useful piece of space infrastructure is an early warning system for hazardous asteroids that could impact Earth with catastrophic results, as well as, the technology to deflect such objects away from Earth. The Obama administration has designated $100 million in NASA's 2014 budget to determine the efficacy of snaring a small asteroid and bringing it to a location where it can be studied. Such a project could tell us much about not only deflecting dangerous asteroids, but how we may take advantage of valuable materials we know that they contain.

The Keck Institute for Space Studies conducted a study at Cal Tech that indicated no launcher more sophisticated than an Atlas V was needed for such an asteroid capture mission. (Keck 2012) However, Senator Nelson is proposing the mission as a use for his favorite "monster rocket". (Nelson 2013) Once again, SLS supporters desperately grasp at anything they can even remotely use as possible justification for it. NASA's true choice is: it can do this mission *very soon* with an *existing* launcher, or twiddle its thumbs *waiting year after year* for SLS and *waste billions* in the process.

If we are to go beyond the Moon and L2 to asteroids or Mars, we will need something more advanced than NASA's Orion-MPCV spacecraft,

SpaceX's Dragonrider spacecraft, Boeing's CST-100 spacecraft, Blue Origin's Biconic spacecraft, or Sierra Nevada's Dream Chaser space-plane.

Working on this problem will require pushing the envelope of human knowledge and developing advanced technologies we currently do not possess. In other words, NASA would *finally* have a high tech challenge *truly worthy* of its vast potential and extraordinary talent pool. Industry cannot properly do it because it is not profitable. It is the kind of thing NASA *used to* excel at before politicians decided they wanted it to build rockets that industry is now capable of doing better, sooner, and more economically. Those politicians' tactics completely ignore the fact that the needed launcher technology *already* exists and companies are *already* structured to produce a high quality, relatively low priced, safe and high reliability vehicle with faster delivery times. If SLS had not been forced on NASA we could use the money wasted on it to develop the cutting-edge interplanetary craft we need for missions to asteroids or Mars *right now*.

The phrase "cutting-edge interplanetary craft", means the first *true* spaceship. In other words, it would be a large vessel which *never* lands on Earth. Crew would travel from Earth in smaller spacecraft made to leave and reenter Earth's atmosphere, such as Dream Chaser, CST-100, and Dragonrider whilst the bigger vessel would take them on exploratory missions into the deep space frontier. Again, there are little known NASA studies that discuss this kind of deep spacecraft, the latest of which holds great promise in addressing the unique dangers such vehicles must be designed to handle. But for now the reader may be asking, "Why are current spacecraft inadequate for this purpose? And what new capabilities will these more advanced spacecraft need?"

For one thing, long term missions relatively close to Earth such as to L2 will require facing dangers to which human beings were never exposed before and thus require new solutions to counter them. The reader may wonder, "We've been to the Moon. Surely we already have *all* the technology we need to go there and survive!" The answer to that assertion is, *no* we did not have *all* of the technology for a *truly practical* level of *long term* safety. That level of safety didn't even exist for the Apollo Moon missions of the 1960's and 70's. In fact, we were damned lucky that the lack of such tech did not result in a dead Moon mission crew.

The main danger is a phenomenon called a *coronal mass ejection* or *CME* for short. This event occurs when the Sun ejects massive amounts of charged particles into space at very high speed in a violent explosion so powerful it makes the energy from a million H-bombs seem like a firecracker. Had one of these eruptions hurled its deadly payload in the direction of the Earth-Moon system during one of the Apollo flights, the brief but intense radiation exposure would have led to an agonizing and hideous death for the astronauts involved. But a relatively quiescent Sun in those years offered low odds of such an event occurring during that particular time. The bet paid off and we got through all the Moon flights without such a horrible accident. But even in such times of minimal solar activity, CMEs still sometimes occur, so in a sense, Lady Luck smiled on Apollo.

Residents of the ISS do not typically need to worry about CMEs because the station orbits below the van Allen radiation belts where the Earth's magnetic field channels most charged particles away from them. The magnetic field lines steer most of the particles towards the Earth's North and South magnetic poles where they may cause an intense display of the Northern and Southern lights when they impact atoms in the atmosphere. Even under normal circumstances, the particles in the belts themselves are of high enough concentration that the Apollo astronauts had to pass through them very fast in order to prevent being exposed to dangerous radiation levels. So the main problem is that continued operations on the Moon, L2 and beyond will require working far away from the protection that the van Allen Belts provide to ISS astronauts and, indeed, to every one of us on planet Earth.

There is also the problem of constant low level cosmic radiation which has deleterious effects on the bodies of even ISS occupants over time.

Another such problem is the harm done to the human body by prolonged time in weightlessness, as I have mentioned earlier.

So the next question is. "Where will all of these new technologies lead us and in what form will they exist?"

5.8 Building the first true spaceship

What is needed is a new kind of fairly large deep-space vessel. This is the kind of exciting groundbreaking project *truly worthy* of the talents of NASA scientists and engineers and doesn't waste their efforts on doing something that has been done for so long and so often that industry can now do it better and cheaper. This space vehicle would have the following characteristics:

1) It can be assembled piecemeal in space from large modular parts lifted from Earth.

2) The constituent parts of the vehicle will be of a size and mass that could be lifted on currently existing launch vehicles rather than a *proposed* new rocket under development such as SLS. Just a fraction of the annual budget being wasted on the development of SLS would be needed to pay for the entire project (as we will see).

3) The vehicle would stay in space and no part of it would ever land on Earth. Crew and passengers are shuttled back and forth between this vehicle and Earth via taxi spacecraft. The smaller taxi craft would be capable of taking off from the ground, reaching the parking orbit of the deep-space vehicle, and re-entering Earth's atmosphere. The current spacecraft being developed under the Commercial Crew project are ideal for this role of taxi.

4) To effectively combat the negative effects of weightlessness on the human body on a long time scale, some kind of "artificial gravity" situation employing spinning of the inhabited part of the spacecraft would be employed.

5) Radiation protection for human travelers would be implemented. This protection would be accomplished with a safe refuge surrounded by the crews' water supply.

6) Preferably an advanced propulsion drive (such as the earlier mentioned VASIMR) would drastically shorten voyage times.

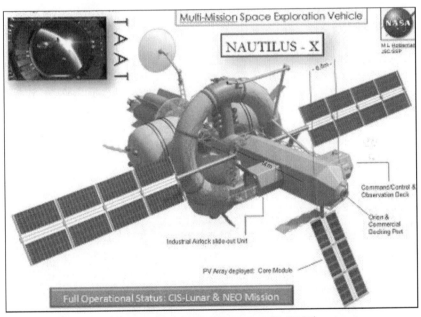

Figure 18: NAUTILUS-X (Image credit: NASA)

A starting point for tackling the project of a large true space vessel is a NASA study of a proposed deep-space vehicle designated the _Non-Atmospheric Universal Transport Intended for Lengthy United States eXploration_ or _NAUTILUS-X_ for short and also alternately known as MMSEV.

(Holderman 2011) The vehicle described in this study addresses five of the six concerns very well, and at least partly applies to point number 2. NAUTILUS-X also shows the lengths to which some engineers will go in order to turn a word into an acronym!

The inadequate addressing of point number 2 (requiring only already existing commercial launchers for assembly of the deep-space vehicle) is the study's Achilles heel. They propose using a combination of already existing vehicles to launch large modules and SLS to launch extremely large modules. Of course, the problem with that approach is:

1) The very cost of development of SLS would tie up money that could be used for the development of the vehicle.

2) Given the *extremely optimistic* supposition that SLS will indeed fly, the *huge* cost per launch of even a *few* launches would detrimentally affect how much budgetary resources could be used to build the deep-space vehicle (even with existing vehicles sharing most of the launch burden).

3) Using SLS for this purpose involves greater risk to the project because a greater percentage of the project's resources will be riding with each single launch of SLS. Losing just one *hyper-expensive* SLS launcher and its crucial cargo would be a major setback for the project. But if a much cheaper and easily replaceable commercial launcher with a smaller less expensive cargo is lost, another rocket can just be pulled out of inventory with the payload being replaced fairly quickly. Alternatively, one of the proposed ULA or SpaceX super launchers could be used if one wanted to keep the parts the same size as they would be for SLS and at the same time be less expensive to develop and operate than SLS.

4) By making a small number of changes to the NASA proposal for NAUTILUS-X, using SLS (whose use would entail the negative financial and time devouring aspects which that launcher entails) or a vehicle of similar payload capacity is totally unnecessary.

So apparently, what we have here is still another instance of vested interests wanting to improperly force the square peg of SLS to fit into yet another inappropriately sized round hole in an attempt to justify that vehicle's existence. Of course, the use of SLS would actually *set back* NAUTILUS or any other American space project. It would happen *not* necessarily because the designers of NAUTILUS-X *want* that negative outcome, but as the result of the vested interests represented by SLS having become institutionalized over a number of decades to such an extent that they are automatically *not questioned* and thus *automatically assumed* to be a benefit rather than a detriment to the Nation's success in spacefaring.

However, even given a hypothetically operational SLS Block 1 added to the mix, it was estimated the *entire* project would cost a total of $3.7 billion dollars (Holderman 2011), or significantly less than two years of SLS's yearly budget. It would be interesting to see what the cost estimate for the project would be with the Block 1 SLS taken out of the mix and with only previously existing launchers used. But of course as long as SLS is being pursued, the money will not be available to do anything with NAUTILUS-X or any other ambitious new deep space project.

5.9 "Farmers", "the Committee" and "Tinkerbells"

As space industry journalist Jeff Foust reported, this institutionally ingrained mentality was aptly described in a talk by former Executive Secretary of the National Space Council under the George H.W. Bush administration, Mark Albrecht:

> *"... his [Mr Albrecht's] current assessment of NASA, in which he suggested the space agency should be "razed and raised", and, more specifically, criticism of the Space Launch System (SLS) heavy-lift rocket, which he said was "too expensive, too slow, and too old.""* (Foust a 2012)

Later in that same article, Jeff goes on to further quote Executive Secretary Albrecht in the following paragraphs:

> *""I think at least three large constituencies have taken hold and own a significant part of NASA and the civil space program," he said, "and they're going to have to be dealt with. As time goes on, as the years go on, they get bigger and stronger and more entrenched."*
> *The first of those constituencies is what Albrecht calls "farmers." These are people "who own a piece of the current program," he said, ranging from a contract or a project all the way to a field center. "They have carved up that $17.3 billion, they lobby for it directly and independently, they fiercely protect it, and anybody who wants to change it is going to have to come through them."*
> *The second group he dubbed "the committee," which represents groups of people who believe that "if you want to do something, every group has to be satisfied," he explained. "So you accept programs, projects, and designs that satisfy the committee requirements, not an efficiently or effectiveness requirement."*
> *The final group in Albrecht's taxonomy is the "Tinkerbells." These are people, he said, who believe that if Americans just knew how great NASA was, "the money would come pouring in and all of these things could be solved."*

The combination of these three groups creates a set of "boundary conditions" that Albrecht said could limit any effort to reform NASA. One is that any new program must be added on top of existing programs, rather than replace them. "If you try to substitute something new for something that's ongoing, we'll get you," he said of those entrenched interests. New programs also have to be contracted in the same, generally cost-plus ways of old programs, he said. (That's why he believes the COTS and CCDev programs, which have used funded Space Act Agreements rather than conventional contracts, have attracted criticism: "Different is threatening, because people start saying, 'why can't you do that differently?' and they don't want to do it differently.") A final boundary condition, according to Albrecht, is that "you have to use, to the maximum extent, the infrastructure that already exists." That means using centers and contractors in their traditional roles.

These constituencies are entrenched within NASA and have to become overcome in order to enable real change for the agency. "The longer it goes, the harder it's going to get because those groups—and there are probably more— get stronger and stronger and stronger." It was those constituencies, he suggested, that stymied the Bush Administration's attempts to focus NASA on the Space Exploration Initiative over 20 years ago." (Foust a 2012)

And Jeff notes the following at the end of the same article (boldface emphasis added by the writer of this book)...

"However, he said he [Albrecht] preferred to find ways to enact what he believes are the necessary changes without slashing NASA's budget. "Let's just think about what we could do with NASA at $17.3 billion, if we really, really focused it, and really got rid of the redundancy," he said. "At $17.3 billion ***we could have an absolutely unbelievable space program."""*** (Foust a 2012)

5.10 Determining who will *honestly* consider the evidence against SLS

It is hoped by the time the reader has reached this far into this book that he/she now has an appreciation for the need for change. It should now be apparent that some parochial Congressional interests together with entrenched institutional inertia in NASA only give certain limited factions advantages in the short run, but *cause harm* to the competiveness of America as *a whole* in the long run. Given that fact, I would like to offer some guidance to those who want to help change along.

As you have seen, a number of people are resisting change simply because they don't know there is a better way and thus their views may be altered by reasonable persuasion. On the other hand, many of those who are heavily invested in the old system (either emotionally, financially or both) will be a hopeless cause. Therefore, it will be helpful for you to be able to identify those people who can be persuaded and those who cannot. From my own interaction and conversations with people who resist needed change, I have noted the following categories of reticent people. My descriptions of their characteristics can help you evaluate whether or not any particular person you encounter is a closed-minded bigot on whom your effort will be wasted because *no amount of reasonable evidence* will ever be enough.

Types of SLS Backers

1) Those who think SLS should be the *only* option and is the *right* option because it is designed by NASA. They also insist SLS *must* be developed in the traditional way, with NASA micromanaging oversight and traditional contracting methods. It is *inconceivable* to these people that anything but the mega rocket Project Apollo paradigm should be followed, because the traditional NASA way of doing things is *holy*. You can't talk someone out of their religion.

2) Super Heavy Lift fans who insist a launch vehicle of Saturn V size or larger is the ONLY way to go. Some of these may be open-minded people who simply might not know about the NASA, industry, and university studies to the contrary and thus can be talked into changing their position. Many of these people may also not realize that if a gargantuan heavy-lift vehicle of SLS's specified power was ever truly needed, then alternatives could be independently developed by commercial launch providers for much less cost than SLS and be safer as well; that is, if certain powerful members of Congress were willing to forego having NASA develop its own vehicle. On the other hand, others will be intractable no matter what, just because the idea goes against what they have accepted as unquestionable truth all their lives and alternate studies saying otherwise will be instantly dismissed (see Type 1). Cost and lost time waiting while the huge new launch vehicle is being developed is also totally ignored by that latter set of people.

3) Shuttle Derived Heavy Lift enthusiasts who think that SDHL is the ONLY way to go. They are essentially a form of the intractable second variant of Type 2. Again, alternate NASA and industry studies saying otherwise are *conveniently ignored*, as are relative costs and lost time waiting for the vehicle's completion.

4) Those who perceive Commercial Crew as a threat to the existence of NASA, even though it can potentially free NASA to pursue

cutting edge technologies to increase the capabilities of humans in LEO, back to the Moon and beyond. Some of these people may be open-minded enough to change their minds *if* their choice of sides is solely due to lack of up-to-date knowledge and not due to fanatical loyalty to the old way of doing things.

5) The NASA Old Guard who either perceive their jobs as being threatened and/or they just don't want the way things have always been done to change. In some cases persuadable, the specifics of which will be discussed at the end of this list.

6) Those who don't like Commercial Crew simply because it has Obama's name associated with it and thus SLS appeals to them as an excuse for taking funds from Commercial Crew by adding those funds to the SLS budget. These people are hopeless because they will not admit *anything* promoted by the Obama administration could *possibly* be good for the Republic.

7) NASA employees working on SLS or those either employed by or associated with a company contracted for SLS and who thus personally benefit from developing SLS.

8) Politicians and others who follow the advice of Types 1 through 7 because SLS economically benefits a particular local area in the short run. They follow this path even though SLS is not in the best interests of the country *as a whole* and also not in the best interests of *any* part of the country *in the long run*. It is possible that some of these people have not had access to valid information which does not support their position, though many of them will just ignore the alternative information simply because they perceive it to counter their *immediate* vested interests.

9) Some just because they haven't taken the time to thoroughly investigate the issue. These people may be the best prospects for reasoned discussion. Indeed, they are the main audience for whom this book was written.

10) Any subset mixture of the above.

A significant fraction of types 1, 2 and 3 are hopelessly unpersuadable because they are religious fanatics, leaving only a small (but open-minded) minority in these groups that one can reason with. Type 6 is just as intractable for a different reason that is just as irrational. It is possible many Type 4s can be won over if they realize what the facts are. Some of Type 5 have opinions set in stone because in certain specific cases there is some basis in reality to their fear of job loss; on the other hand, others of this type might change because they would flourish under the new paradigm but they just don't realize it yet. Pure Type 7 people are as unchangeable as the most adamant of those people who fit types 1, 2, 3 and 6, but at least they have a rational reason. Some of Type 8 can eventually change when they realize that even though the new paradigm may have some negative effects for their local area in the short run, it will be a net plus in the long run. Many pure Type 9s with no personal axe to grind (that is, with none of the worst Type 1, 2, 3 and 6 tendencies) may change their position when presented with the facts.

A minority of SLS backers are purely only one of the types 1 through 9, with most being some form of Type 10 admixture. Of course, any particular form of a Type 10 person will only be changeable as long they also don't possess any of the most fanatical mindsets that often are found in types 1, 2, 3 and 6, and also don't exhibit Type 7.

5.11 What is really important to insure American space supremacy?

Ultimately, whether or not a person is persuadable depends to what extent he/she accepts the importance of all of the four important precepts of those people who both *actually* know what is going on and who also *really* care about having Americans go <u>BLEO</u> (<u>beyond low Earth orbit</u>). Those precepts are:

1) The vehicles sending our astronauts to space (whether LEO or BLEO) should be American made. We don't care what particular Americans make those vehicles as long as it results in a significant increase in American spaceflight (something SLS can't do).
2) That we go beyond LEO *as soon as possible*. (With SLS, we have to wait for the launch vehicle to be developed, instead of using existing launch vehicles to get started *now*).
3) Not waste the hard earned money of the taxpayer (With SLS we have to spend more to do less or even *nothing*).
4) Make sure that whatever vehicles we choose are as safe as fallible humans can make them.

The best way to accomplish *all* four of those goals is through the mechanism that has traditionally given America its enormous economic strength. Not long ago we finished decades of a Cold War in which we proclaimed to the world our system of competition through a private free enterprise system was superior to an opposing system where big centrally controlled government agencies mandated the production of everything the society needed. Our space program is one of the few areas where we have not practiced what we have always preached by implementing the equivalent of Soviet design bureau that minutely oversees the design and development of a product from beginning to end without worrying about minimizing cost. NASA's former head of Commercial Space, Charles Miller states the case well:

> *"We should completely privatize all US launch systems. The process of privatization started over 25 years ago, when Ronald Reagan removed commercial satellites from the Space Shuttle in 1986 by executive order. It continued when a Democratic Congress passed the Launch Services Purchase Act of 1990, which was signed by a Republican President. Then, again, when a Republican Congress passed the Commercial Space Act of 1998, which was signed by a Democratic President. Finally, a second President Bush proposed the Commercial Crew and Cargo program in 2004, and President Obama made it his top space policy priority.*
> *The government does not design or develop airplanes, or trucks, or trains, and it should not be designing launch vehicles."* (Miller 2013)

Now that the reader knows what is possible without SLS and the evidence that may be used as counterpoints against its continuation, perhaps it is the time to turn our focus toward how well the transition from Shuttle to Commercial Crew is proceeding, the political strategies still being used to impede that transition to the advantage of SLS, and Commercial Crew's advantages over its Shuttle predecessor.

Chapter 6: The transition to the Commercial Cargo and Commercial Crew Programs

"America will always do the right thing, but only after exhausting all other options."
-- Winston Churchill[4]

"Some minds remain open long enough for the truth not only to enter, but to pass on through by way of a ready exit without pausing anywhere along the route."
-- Sister Elizabeth Kenny – founder of modern physical rehabilitation therapy

"Hell is paved with good intentions, not bad ones."
-- George Bernard Shaw -- from Man and Superman

It is common knowledge that the Commercial Cargo program for hauling cargo to and from the ISS (using launchers and spacecraft available on the commercial market) was promoted and instituted at the higher levels of the G.W. Bush administration. Though the Obama administration has been actively pursuing the Commercial Crew route for sending American astronauts to and from the ISS, many would be surprised to know that there was serious consideration of instituting that method of crew transportation within the G.W. Bush administration. However, resistance within the traditional NASA upper level administration and from certain influential politicians was so strong that it caused leading promoters of the commercialization of space flight within the Bush administration to only press for the Commercial Cargo option. They were in a very similar situation to what the Obama administration is now with respect to Commercial Crew and SLS: accept some progress rather than none at all.

---

[4] Stevenson, Tom; 2011; "Let us hope that the US realises quite what a mess it's in", *The Telegraph*, London, UK, July 23
http://www.telegraph.co.uk/finance/comment/tom-stevenson/8656616/Let-us-hope-that-the-US-realises-quite-what-a-mess-its-in.html

I could go into detail about the political ins and outs that led to the decision not to institute a Commercial Crew style program during the G.W. Bush administration, but the focus of this book is about issues that need to be addressed *now* to tackle the related problems of obstructionist politicians and intransigent mid-level and upper-level management within NASA. In fact, if the Commercial Crew route had been actively pursued as early as it was originally proposed rather than Ares-1, our country might not be spending as many years in the current *humiliating* situation of having its astronauts hauled to the ISS solely on Russian vehicles. What's more, much of the Commercial Crew concept has its roots in several previous administrations of decades past and there is enough material in that vein alone for another entire book.

But the important thing for now is that the Commercial Crew ball has been picked up and run with. Because of that, we now have a chance to break out of the vicious cycle of super expensive hardware development which has kept astronauts in low Earth orbit during all the decades since Apollo. So the current implementation of Commercial Crew is a perfect example of Churchill's assertion. But there are still powerful forces arrayed to minimize its effects and who strive to make discontinuation of SLS as difficult as possible.

6.1 A power grab to protect the pork

Six Congressional representatives (Reps. John Culberson, Frank Wolf, Bill Posey, Pete Olson, James Sensenbrenner and Lamar Smith) introduced legislation called *The Space Leadership Act*. (Posey 2012) The general consensus among many space policy experts is that this proposal is a reaction to the cancellation of Project Constellation by the Obama administration with the intent of stripping any future President of the ability to terminate similar space program related boondoggles. According to these experts, the introduction of this bill is especially in response to the removal from office of the former NASA administrator who was the driving force behind Project Constellation and who strove to keep it going despite massive cost overruns that necessitated taking funds from other NASA projects to feed the ravenous maw of Ares-1 and Orion development. (Smith a 2012)

Of course, these representatives tried their best to put a noble face on their effort before the public. For instance, when proposing the legislation, the sponsoring lawmakers presented a chart with misleading and inaccurate information in an effort to cast it in as favorable a light as possible. Proof of the lack of validity of the information contained in the chart is explained in an excellent article by space issues reporter Doug Messier. (Messier b 2012)

Details of the proposed legislation are as follows:

1) It stipulates the creation of a Board of Directors that would be chosen by the administration, House, and Senate, consisting of former astronauts and noted scientists with each board member serving up to three three-year terms.

2) The board would determine NASA's proposed budget for each year.

3) The board would recommend people for the positions of NASA Administrator, Assistant Administrator and Chief Financial Officer.

4) The administrator would serve a 10 year term.

5) The board would have the power to remove an administrator.

During the announcement of the proposed legislation, the Congressmen bemoaned what they termed was the wasting of billions of dollars when Project Constellation was canceled by the Obama administration. (Smith a 2012) But as Stephen C. Smith reminds us in his article regarding the legislation's introduction:

> *"Apparently no mention was made of the several GAO audits prior to 2009 which concluded that Constellation was years behind schedule, billions over budget and "lacked a sound business case".* *"* (Smith a 2012)

Mr. Smith's contention is indeed bolstered by United States Government Accountability Office findings. (GAO 2009) Yes, there was indeed a wasting of billions of dollars, though not because of the cancellation of Constellation as the Congressmen claimed, but due to the inherent makeup and development procedures of the project itself. Given that fact, it *appears* all the good Congressmen wanted was to make sure any space-related pork they might want to get behind in the future could not be blocked by the Executive Branch, rather than a genuine concern with maintaining the Nation's "Space Leadership". Thus, the official name the good Congressmen gave to this proposed legislation is the ultimate oxymoron and a pinnacle of Orwellian double-speak, prompting the bill's opponents to refer to it by the more apt moniker of *The Space Anti-Leadership Act*.

This less than fruitful effort was not enough to stop the good Congressmen from trying again. In February 2013, a slightly modified version of the act was reintroduced. It too was not enacted. The irony is a committee *already exists* whose purpose is to monitor and scrutinize "the long-term goals, core capabilities, and direction" of NASA human spaceflight: the National Research Council's *Committee on Human Spaceflight* which was commissioned by Congress a few years ago. (National Academy of Sciences 2013) It then appears that the new legislation is an attempt at creating an alternate committee that the aforesaid group of Congressmen could more easily set up to do their bidding than would the currently existing Committee on Human Spaceflight.

To support the assertion made in the preceding paragraph, following is a verbatim quote of the Committee on Human Spaceflight's formally assigned "Statement of Task":

> *"In accordance with Section 204 of the NASA Authorization Act 2010, the National Research Council (NRC) will appoint an ad hoc committee to undertake a study to review the long-term goals, core capabilities, and direction of the U.S. human spaceflight program and make recommendations to enable a sustainable U.S. human spaceflight program.*
>
> *The committee will:*
>
> *1. Consider the goals for the human spaceflight program as set forth in (a) the National Aeronautics and Space Act of 1958, (b) the National Aeronautics and Space Administration Authorization Acts of 2005, 2008, and 2010, and (c) the National Space Policy of the United States (2010), and any existing statement of space policy issued by the president of the United States.*
>
> *2. Solicit broadly-based, but directed, public and stakeholder input to understand better the motivations, goals, and possible evolution of human spaceflight--that is, the foundations of a rationale for a compelling and sustainable U.S. human spaceflight program--and to characterize its value to the public and other stakeholders.*
>
> *3. Describe the expected value and value proposition of NASA's human spaceflight activities in the context of national goals--including the needs of government, industry, the economy, and the public good--and in the context of the priorities and programs of current and potential international partners in the spaceflight program.*
>
> *4. Identify a set of high-priority enduring questions that describe the rationale for and value of human exploration in a national and international context. The questions should motivate a sustainable direction for the long-term exploration of space by humans. The enduring questions may include scientific, engineering, economic, cultural, and social science questions to be addressed by human space exploration and questions on improving the overall human condition.*
>
> *5. Consider prior studies examining human space exploration, and NASA's work with international partners, to understand possible exploration pathways (including key technical pursuits and destinations) and the appropriate balance between the "technology push" and "requirements pull". Consideration should include the analysis completed by NASA's Human Exploration Framework Team, NASA's Human Spaceflight Architecture Team, the Review of U.S.*

Human Spaceflight Plans (Augustine Commission), previous NRC reports, and relevant reports identified by the committee.

6. Examine the relationship of national goals to foundational capabilities, robotic activities, technologies, and missions authorized by the NASA Authorization Act of 2010 by assessing them with respect to the set of enduring questions.

7. Provide findings, rationale, prioritized recommendations, and decision rules that could enable and guide future planning for U.S. human space exploration. The recommendations will describe a high-level strategic approach to ensuring the sustainable pursuit of national goals enabled by human space exploration, answering enduring questions, and delivering value to the nation over the fiscal year (FY) period of FY2014 through FY2023, while considering the program's likely evolution in 2015-2030.

This project is being funded by NASA." (National Academy of Sciences 2013)

6.2 The Congressional propaganda smokescreen

But the so-called "Space Leadership Act" was just one instance of the political spin doctoring the mentioned Congressmen have put forward. Some of them have taken actions in defense of SLS with attempts to keep the budget of Commercial Crew as low as possible in order to maximize the money available for SLS development. To illustrate the truth of this assertion, I will start by giving to you a statement from Representative Posey's testimony before the House Budget Committee:

"Unfortunately, the President's proposed budget is a substantial departure from the Authorization Bill that he signed into law in October--cutting $2 billion from the heavy lift program while increasing taxpayer subsidies for the low earth orbit commercial space companies." (Cowing a 2011)

There are a couple of points to be made about Rep. Posey's quote above. First, the $2 billion he said the Administration wanted to cut from SLS was money that in a prior year's budget proposal was originally slated for Commercial Crew by the Administration. On the contrary, the Administration was trying to *restore* funds they had originally planned for Commercial Crew, but which had been instead used by Senate and House committee members in order to maximize SLS related pork in the final budget bill of the previous year. Furthermore, if one looks at the meaning of the word *subsidy*, the development of SLS comes a lot closer to fitting that definition than Commercial Crew vehicle development does. As *Merriam-Webster's Collegiate® Dictionary, Eleventh Edition* defines the word:

"Subsidy - … a grant by a government to a private person or company to assist an enterprise deemed advantageous to the public"[5]

At best one could say Commercial Crew development is a *partial* subsidy since the government pays for only a *fraction* of the development cost of the vehicles in that program. Contrast that setup to the *total* subsidy related to SLS where the private contractor companies working on the development of the vehicle are compensated for *100%* of their costs and a *hefty* profit besides, *even in the event of failure.*

But before all of the above mentioned ploys were attempted, some of these politicians were conducting a concerted effort to force NASA to choose only one Commercial Crew vehicle provider instead of having a true competition. The idea was to free the maximum amount of NASA budget money for SLS. As was written earlier, they have met with partial success by getting the funded participants cut down to three. Before discussing the details of the political maneuvering which took place in obtaining that dubious achievement, now is probably a good time for an in-depth discussion about the disadvantages of paring down Commercial Crew participants. To understand the most significant aspects of this issue, we need to look at some of the characteristics of the Space Shuttle these new vehicles are to replace in its crew transportation capacity.

6.3 Advantages of multiple Commercial Crew participants

One of the biggest drawbacks of the Shuttle was that NASA had all of its metaphorical space transportation "eggs" in one vehicle "basket". Reliance on only one vehicle meant that if any kind of problem manifested itself and the vehicle had to be taken out of service while the problem was resolved, the U.S. would be stranded without a way to get its astronauts into space. Indeed, this is what happened after both the Challenger and Columbia accidents.

In the airline industry, the American flying public is not stranded in cases where an accident happens to a particular model of airplane while the cause of the accident is being investigated. Instead, there are other types of airliner available on which people can ride while investigators try to find out if there is an inherent danger in a particular aircraft and, if so, how to

---

[5] By permission. From *Merriam-Webster's Collegiate® Dictionary, Eleventh Edition* ©2012 by Merriam-Webster, Incorporated (www.Merriam-Webster.com)

fix the problem. This kind of redundancy is one of the advantages that multiple Commercial Crew vehicles offer us in human spaceflight. If a particular model of vehicle is grounded, our nation would no longer find itself in the *embarrassing* position of relying exclusively on another country's space transportation hardware. Instead, other *American* manufacturers' vehicles would take up the slack.

While Russia and America are no longer as antagonistic as they were during the Cold War, their interests and ours often do not coincide. For instance, they sometimes intimidate their immediate neighbors and, as their invasion of Georgia in 2008 illustrates, are not above doing so militarily. What if another such incident occurs? Would the U.S. protest it as vigorously as it should with the threat of Russia cancelling our taxi service to ISS? Given that propensity, how can any responsible American politician prefer giving more money to SLS over Commercial Crew when keeping the latter at a minimum budget amount irresponsibly *increases* the time we precariously rely on the Russians?

As stated by space industry consultant Rick Tumlinson (cofounder of the *Space Frontier Foundation*):

> *"... let's use the $38 billion Congress wants to flush down the toilet of history to save NASA by funding useful programs that will actually open the frontier and get the agency back to exploring almost right away.*
> *Yes, the priority right now is transportation. But not some overpriced monster rocket that won't fly for a decade (if ever) while we pay the Russians $60 million per flight to carry our people to the space station.*
> *As insane as it sounds, Congress is strangling NASA's plans to end this outsourcing and use U.S. commercial rockets through its Commercial Crew Development program, cutting the already measly $800 million allocation to around $300 million."* (Tumlinson 2011)

Another significant drawback in having only one vehicle supplier is that there is little incentive for a manufacturer to keep prices down, since there would be no competitors applying market pressure. As the sole supplier, a manufacturer can charge the maximum price he thinks his customer can afford because said customer is at a severe disadvantage from having no other source from which to buy. So by trying to strip Commercial Crew down to the minimum, the political perpetrators are potentially disabling much of the program's advantage to the taxpayer.

But perhaps the best result of having numerous vehicle providers is the creation of a new private space industry that could become a major stimulus to the Nation's economy. For instance, as mentioned earlier a company called Bigelow Aerospace has been waiting for years for the commercially available launchers it needs to economically put their space stations into orbit and also spacecraft to send people to them. Hardly some pie-in-the-sky (pun intended) scheme, since Bigelow has had two prototype space stations with full internal environmental control in orbit for years now. (Bigelow 2012) Furthermore, a number of nations have signed agreements of intent with the company. (David 2010) Think about it, literally billions of dollars could be infused into our country's economy from other nations via the sale of *American made* launchers, spacecraft and space stations! That would be sure to help our balance of trade. Even more economic stimulus would also come from the purchase of flights by *domestic* companies that need affordable orbital research stations or tourist destinations.

For those who would suggest that selling our commercial space technology to other countries will put us at a security disadvantage, they should be reminded that we already sell *our most advanced weapons* to our allies. Given that the countries with whom Bigelow is dealing are longtime friends such as the Britain, Netherlands, Australia, Singapore, Japan and Sweden (who already get *our best* and most advanced defense hardware and systems), this argument has a very hollow ring to it. (David 2010)

But not only will the launchers used in Commercial Crew be used for sending both people and cargo to ISS and private space stations, they will be launching commercial satellites and robotic space probes as well. The result is an even higher volume of launches of the same rockets, *which will drive launch costs down even further.*

The point is: the greater the number of American spaceflight hardware suppliers available, the more resilient the new private space industry will be. Over the years there has been a real problem getting certain members of Congress to either understand that fact or acknowledge it. Regardless of how many times they hear logical arguments to the contrary of what they want to believe, their minds are fast moving freeways that good ideas flow into and almost instantly egress in much the same manner described by Sister Elizabeth Kenny.

6.4 The Commercial Crew down-selection effort

Representative Tom Wolf of Virginia is a prime example of such a politician. For a long time Rep. Wolf had urged that Commercial Crew be pared down to only one entrant to maximize funds available for SLS. He and others would often use the argument that Commercial Crew contenders' reliability was questionable. However, after SpaceX's success with getting cargo to the ISS under the Commercial Cargo program with Falcon 9 and Dragon, it was evident cutting Commercial Crew to the bone was no longer an option that would be politically acceptable. He then put forward the proposal of financing development of three contestants rather than all of the five that were funded at that time. (Klingler b 2012)

Rep. Posey was also initially an advocate of extreme down-selecting in the Commercial Crew program. In defense of this position as well as more money for SLS, here are his very words:

> *"Do you hire one contractor to build your $100,000 house? Or do you hire four contractors and say, see how far you can go for $25,000 each?"* (Foust b 2012)

Of course, such a remark shows a completely oblivious attitude in relation to the true reasons for the existence of Commercial Crew as I have previously outlined them. As in the case of Mr. Wolf, Mr. Posey has had to come to grips with not stripping Commercial Crew down as far as he would like by going along with shrinking it to two fully funded competitors plus one at half funding. But, as of the time of the publication of this book, both Representatives are still trying to route the maximum amount of funds to SLS that they can get away with.

6.5 SLS, Commercial Crew and the sequester

As I write this book, the dreaded budget sequester went into effect by default. Already word is going out that both Commercial Crew and SLS will receive a cut. Right now while this book is being written, it appears Commercial Crew will be cut from $525 million to $480 million. If this indeed occurs, there can only be three possible outcomes, the budget sequester will: 1) set back the time American launch providers will take over from the Russians and 2) be the excuse Commercial Crew opponents need to pare down the number of participants even further, or 3) lead to a combination of both the first two options. In other words, some politicians would rather pay extra hundreds of millions of dollars to a foreign country than fix the Russian reliance problem by cancelling a project (SLS) for which the Nation *has absolutely no practical use* and applying *a small part* of the funds from the latter to the more useful former. (Foust e 2013) The other part of the freed up funds could be used for the technology research and interplanetary exploration projects covered in Chapter 5 in this book.

6.6 SLS and the Chinese

Both Representatives Wolf and Posey cite the prospect of a Moon landing by the Chinese followed by a subsequent total takeover of that closest nearby world as a reason for the continued development of SLS. (Wolf 2011; Posey b 2011) Of course, as the evidence laid out earlier in this book indicates, pursuing SLS would practically insure that the Chinese would indeed beat us back to Moon or any other deep space destination because it is the *slowest* and *most expensive* way to accomplish that purpose. Indeed, going that route would probably mean *not* going back to the lunar surface *at all* for reasons already outlined.

The good representatives; however, claim the Chinese are developing a huge heavy-lift booster with a payload capacity that is the similar to what SLS Block 2 would have. (Wolf 2011; Smith b 2012) Indeed, there have been studies made by the Chinese that have produced plans for building such a rocket (Zhang 2011), but no formal commencement of development of such a vehicle has happened up to the time of the writing of this book, nor even a formal announcement from the Chinese government of the development of such a vehicle.

I'm not saying the following scenario is *actually* occurring, but if the Chinese are really smart about wanting to retard the U.S. in space, they could put out information that their government is developing a gargantuan rocket in order to *make sure* our country continues to go along SLS's dead-end path. This strategy would allow the Chinese to follow more practical means of doing deep space exploration (such as the alternatives I have covered) while America spins its metaphorical wheels wasting money on SLS.

Alternatively, it could also be the Chinese are as stuck in the old conventional mindset of the Apollo style heavy-lifter as many in America are. This scenario would be a plus for us even if their enormous rocket actually got built under the cumbersome guidance of a large government bureaucracy using inefficient contracting methods with work spread over many agency centers and contractors (similar to SLS development). Just as with our Apollo program, they would *at most* only be able to land on the Moon a few times because the launch vehicle's operational economic impracticality in the long term would be its undoing (as happened to us with Apollo). All they would end up with is a short-lived "flags and footprints" repeat of America's Apollo lunar expeditions: a ho hum "me too" accomplishment with no real payoff other than indicating to the world that China "has arrived" as a space power and also some possible new scientific knowledge about the Moon.

I am not stating as ironclad fact that the Chinese are actually taking either of the above stated paths, but if they *are* serious about going to Moon, then they *have to be* choosing one of those two ways or the other. If they are, we can only *hope* Wolf and Posey are correct on this one point and their choice is the same ineffective path that is being championed by SLS supporters.

What facts indicate the enormous Chinese government-industrial aerospace complex would probably not be able to develop an *economically viable* huge launcher any more than NASA could? Well, they are already highly disturbed because they cannot get their price per kilogram to orbit down to what SpaceX is charging for a Falcon 9 launcher with payload capacities roughly comparable to the mass that their best current vehicles can launch. (Cowing c 2011) That would lead one to the conclusion they probably couldn't get the development cost of their SLS sized launcher down to anywhere near the $2.5 billion development cost SpaceX has quoted for that size launch vehicle. Furthermore, it wouldn't be a surprise if they couldn't even match ULA's $5.5 billion estimate, given the inefficiencies introduced by China's big government development project similar to SLS. After development, the price per launch would probably be prohibitively high as well due to a combination of higher regular production costs per launch vehicle and the amortization of the huge development costs on a per launch basis. The founder and CEO of SpaceX, Elon Musk, summed up the situation nicely:

> *"China has the fastest growing economy in the world. But the American free enterprise system, which allows anyone with a better mouse-trap to compete, is what will ensure that the United States remains the world's greatest superpower of innovation."* (Musk 2011)

There are Republicans (such as Representative *Dana Rohrabacher*, former Executive Secretary of the Space Council *Mark Albrecht*, and former Reagan administration policy assistant for Science and Technology *Jim Muncy*) who are not hypocritical when it comes to following their party's long stated preference for letting the forces of *true* free competition wield their economic strength to the benefit of the Nation's economy. Unfortunately, there are also Republicans such as Wolf and Posey who behave as though they think this historically powerful mechanism only works for pursuing goals beneath the atmosphere, but not for goals in space.

The main point of the previous paragraph is that even though most of the public figures of whom I have been less than complimentary are Republican, that condition is not due to rabid anti-Republicanism on my part, but merely stems from the *demographic fact* that the *vast majority* of representatives of the traditional space states are Republican. Because of their vested interest in space-related issues, politicians of *both major* parties from these states have made an extra effort to gain positions on the powerful House and Senate committees and subcommittees overseeing these issues. What we have is a case of the foxes guarding the NASA budget henhouse.

In order to give *the appearance* of assuaging the concern that SLS was being built without competitive bidding, it was decided that the boosters for the Block 1B and Block 2 versions of SLS would be open for

99

competition. (Bergin c 2012) However, this decision does not address the true objection to the way SLS is being developed; that objection is *the whole vehicle* should be competed with a number of companies putting forward *their own* vehicle designs and bids. Competing only the boosters might lead to *some* savings during development, but the main source of expense for SLS is the way the vehicle *as a whole* is being developed *not* the way any particular *part* of it is being developed. The reasons why this is true have already been laid out earlier in this book. Again, the pseudo-competition ploy appears to be an attempt to give *the impression* extensive competition is occurring where it is not and in turn supplies a rationale to justify the continued development of SLS via traditional cost and payment structures.

But don't think it's only House members who are trying to politically finesse the continuation of SLS at any cost to the detriment of the Commercial Crew program …

Senator Hutchison left her Senate seat at the end of 2012, but before stepping down from her position she executed a crafty questionable legislative maneuver she hoped would allow her to make SLS invulnerable from beyond the political grave. She tried to put an amendment (S.A. 3078) into a Defense Authorization Bill (S. 3254) that stated the following:

> *"(e) LEVEL OF EFFORT ASSURANCE.—*
> *(1) IN GENERAL.—To ensure sufficient resources for the development of Federal and*
> *commercial launch capabilities under titles III and IV of the National Aeronautics and*
> *Space Administration Authorization Act of 2010 (42 U.S.C. 18301 et seq.; 124 Stat. 2805), for fiscal years 2014 and 2015 the proportionate funding levels for the Space Launch System, the Multi-Purpose Crew Vehicle, known as Orion, and related Ground Systems and technology developments, shall be no less than the proportion as provided in the aggregate within the Exploration account for fiscal year 2013.*
> *(2) EXCEPTION.—Paragraph (1) shall not apply if the amounts provided for the activities under paragraph (1) for fiscal year 2014 or fiscal year 2015 are equal to or greater than the aggregate amounts provided for each of those activities for fiscal year 2012 or 2013, whichever is greater, by an Act of Congress."* (Foust f 2012)

Obviously, this was an attempt to insure that in the event NASA's budget is cut, SLS and Orion would not be cut. In that situation, the only way cuts to those two projects could be avoided would be by cannibalizing funds from Commercial Crew and much needed new technology development. (Foust f 2012) The bill being amended concerned *military* spending which is normally *unrelated* to NASA (a *civilian* agency of the government), but stretching the limits beyond customary legislative procedure to accomplish her desired end was apparently not a concern for her. Fortunately for the future of the NASA human spaceflight program, the proposed bill to which she added the amendment only passed as a non-binding "Sense of Congress" recommendation and thus did not have the force of law behind it.

6.7 Congressional SLS supporters unknowingly harm their constituents

What is truly ironic about the positions of the previously mentioned politicians (who would either slow down or eliminate Commercial Crew to keep SLS at full funding) is that it appears they don't realize that their constituents and the rest of the country would actually be better off *in the long run* with the elimination of SLS and increasing funding of new technologies for deep space exploration. Given this fact one can only posit that this situation must be due to bad advice from one or more trusted staff members.

Take the Congressional representative of the Space Coast of Florida, Mr. Posey, favoring funds for SLS over Commercial Crew as an example. As has already been shown, even given the dubious proposition that it ever flies, SLS would probably only launch a couple of times a year at most. Launches have always been a big tourist draw to the part of Florida he represents. While Commercial Crew launches for NASA could occur much more often than Shuttle launches did in the past, there would also be an even greater volume of launches to Bigelow space stations and other commercial operations. The much greater volume of flights would be a steady tourist draw throughout the year rather than an occasional flight every half year or so. Imagine the enormous increase in tourist revenue that could result from such regular and frequent launches.

In the case of Senator Hutchison, transferring funds from Commercial Crew to SLS is also counter to the best interests of the Texas residents she represented. Remember former high level NASA executives Chris Kraft and Tom Moser pointed out SLS is actually a bad deal for people whose livelihood depends on NASA's Johnson Space Center in Houston. (Kraft & Moser 2012) But beyond the criticisms those two gentleman posed, for years before Hutchison left her Senatorial seat, SpaceX has had an extensive and highly active rocket engine testing facility in McGregor, Texas that pumps many millions of dollars into the economy around McGregor. Then there is the fact that SpaceX may be building its large private spaceport near Brownsville, Texas for its own unrestricted use to make it easier for them to meet the very high volume of launches that they anticipate. That spaceport would probably not only bring in money directly from contracted launches, but from tourists eager to see the lift-off of large rockets. Falcon Heavy launches from Brownsville should be *spectacular* and *a very big tourist draw*, since that rocket will have more power than the Shuttle had; indeed, it will be the most powerful rocket since the Saturn V moon rocket!

Perhaps the most ardent attempted suppressor of Commercial Crew and proponent of SLS is Senator Richard Shelby of Alabama, now ranking member of the powerful Senate Appropriations Committee. His efforts to stifle Commercial Crew are legendary within the space community. In fact, here in his own words is his view of it, an opinion which is founded on a belief in a number of the myths mentioned in Chapter 2 of this book:

> ""*I believe NASA would better serve the American taxpayer by continuing to push the frontiers of human space travel in its own right," said Sen. Richard Shelby (R-Ala.) "There are no 'private' space companies; only taxpayer-funded ones that NASA has arbitrarily decided to call 'commercial' and hold to reduced standards of performance and accountability."* " (Hennigan 2012)

Shelby had earlier backed up these words with action. He and Senator Bob Bennett of Utah sponsored an amendment to a bill to keep spending money on Ares-1 after the Obama administration called for its cancellation. Their plan was to get part of the money to do the extension of Ares-1 from funds approved for Commercial Crew. This move prompted the watchdog organization *Citizens Against Public Waste* to bestow upon Mr. Shelby the dubious honor of *Porker of the Month.* (Matthews c 2010)

But even earlier, he had tried to cripple Commercial Crew before it even started. Portraying it as though SpaceX would be the only beneficiary of the program, Shelby had $150 million removed from Commercial Crew back when it was formally known as COTS-D. (Foust d 2009) He did this even though it was well known that ULA would be building Atlas V rocket launchers in Decatur, Alabama which would be used to launch some of the Commercial Crew spacecraft. During the early COTS-D days of Commercial Crew, Elon Musk expressed some puzzlement over Shelby's position:

> "*The CEO of a company seeking to carry American astronauts into space says U.S. Sen. Richard Shelby, R-Tuscaloosa, is fighting a new national space plan that would bring billions into North Alabama.*
> "*I just don't understand what his beef is," Elon Musk, CEO of Space Exploration Technologies Inc. (SpaceX) said in a telephone interview Friday night.*
> "*I don't really understand why Sen. Shelby is so opposed to commercial crew," Musk said, "given that Atlas and Delta are right there in Alabama, because*

no one's going to be a bigger winner in commercial crew than United Launch Alliance."'" (Roop 2010)

Since it was well known to politicians that Commercial Crew spacecraft would be launched on ULA rockets as well as SpaceX rockets, the good Senator apparently thought that the Huntsville produced SLS is good enough for launching people but Commercial Crew launchers are not. Given that fact, does it mean he doesn't believe the rockets produced by his constituents in Decatur are as good as rockets developed by his Huntsville constituents? It makes one wonder.

Another point Senator Shelby doesn't seem to understand is that the commercial space companies **need** the Marshall Spaceflight Center in Huntsville and put money into Alabama's economy that way. The companies **pay** to use the testing facilities at Marshall. For example, during their *Grasshopper* program for developing a reusable launcher, SpaceX has had Marshall conduct wind tunnel tests to get valuable data on how a reusable Falcon 9 first stage booster would behave during atmospheric reentry. (Newton a 2012) No doubt SpaceX will need similar tests run for the second stage booster as well.

Marshall is also conducting tests of the launch abort system for the SpaceX Dragonrider manned spacecraft along with doing work on SpaceX's on-orbit propulsion systems. The expert engineers at Marshall are also providing SpaceX with expertise related to spacecraft attitude and control. Furthermore, they are helping SpaceX by providing invaluable assistance in the development of "materials and processes" needed for future versions of SpaceX launchers and spacecraft. (Newton a 2012)

But it's not just SpaceX bringing cash into Alabama this way. Marshall also has done wind tunnel testing on Sierra Nevada's Dream Chaser spacecraft. (Newton b 2012)

Finally, Senator Shelby should realize that if SLS was cancelled, Marshall and other NASA centers would still have plenty to do developing the *new* technologies America would need in the *revitalization* of the exploration program which that cancellation would enable. There could be a boost in funding to the advanced propulsion projects getting just a trickle of funding now, such as VASIMR. These technologies would leap frog our country far ahead of everyone else in space exploration if they were accelerated significantly. But as long as SLS exists to keep Senator Shelby's Marshall constituents working on old-style rocket launchers that do not do justice to NASA's more state-of the-art capabilities, the wherewithal won't exist to give those people the opportunity to lay the groundwork for a truly useful spacefaring future.

At the time of the writing of this book, Senator Shelby still favors SLS at the expense of Commercial Crew. He and his fellow SLS supporters continue to ignore the fact that SLS would be *the least practical* option, even if a huge heavy lifter was truly needed. Evidence already presented herein shows it isn't needed, but for the sake of argument, what if a heavy lift vehicle of SLS's throw weight was indeed a necessity for *any kind* of deep space exploration? In that case, why not use one of the other possible heavy-lift alternatives?

As I have already pointed out, ULA and SpaceX both quoted estimated total costs of launchers with payload capacity equaling or exceeding the payload capacity of SLS Block 2 and those quoted estimates were many billions of dollars less than *the most optimistic* projected total development costs for SLS. Does Senator Shelby not see that Marshall would be needed in the development of these rockets too? We could actually pay for *both* alternative launchers to be developed *for far less than* what is going down the SLS rabbit hole **and** still have money left over for development of new groundbreaking technologies besides! Furthermore, as shown earlier within these pages, once these alternative vehicles were flying they would cost *much less* to operate than SLS. But as was also indicated, though the U.S. may *eventually* need an enormous heavy-lift launch vehicle, in the meantime we can send our astronauts on ambitious deep space explorations with already existing launchers (according to NASA's own study).

6.8 ASAP recommendations that could harm American space leadership

Now that sufficient attention has been given to what has been going on within the chambers and halls of Congress, it is time to turn our attention to more actions of ASAP that could affect the future of the Commercial Crew effort. First, I would like to draw attention to the following passage from that body's report for the year 2012:

> *"A key aspect of the CCP [Commercial Crew Program] is the acquisition strategy. NASA originally planned to implement a two-part certification process using Federal Acquisition Regulation (FAR)-based contracts, with the first part being an integrated design contract and the second part focusing on development, test, evaluation, and certification. However, because the funding provided was only about half of the requested level, NASA decided to use SAAs for the first part, CCiCap. The second part, involving the actual certification work, was still to be performed under a FAR-based contract. Based on concerns expressed by the ASAP and others that there could be a major disconnect between the systems developed under SAAs and the systems needed to meet NASA's certification requirements under a contract, NASA recently modified its acquisition strategy to add a Certification Products Contract (CPC) in parallel with the development work being accomplished*

under CCiCap. This new certification approach (see Figure 1), carried out under FAR-based contracts, will be executed in two phases: the first phase, the CPC, will allow earlier formal discussions between NASA and the partners on exactly what deviations from NASA certification requirements, if any, would be requested and allowed; and the second phase, the Certification Contract, will provide the validation, verification, testing, and final certification in order to complete the process. We believe that the Phase 1/Phase 2 certification approach helps to clear the certification "fog" and is a significant step forward." (Dyer a et al. 2013)

There are several points worth noting in the above excerpt from the ASAP report. First, the part mentioning that NASA "originally planned" a FAR based system for Commercial Crew vehicle development is not correct. The Commercial Crew Program was created and the first larger number of commercial participants was selected *before* the FAR based system was chosen. In other words, *the program was begun before FAR was chosen* **for any part of it**. In fact, the CCP participants were hoping for and (more or less expected) an SAA based system in that early period before the announcement of using FAR, an announcement which was made on July 20, 2011 during NASA's first Commercial Crew Program Forum. That forum consisted of a panel of three NASA officials who made the announcement along with a live studio audience who were representatives of the selected Commercial Crew participants and other concerned companies. The reader can actually witness everything that transpired during this forum in an online video from NASA. The web link needed to access the video is listed in the reference cited at the end of this sentence. (NASA b 2011) Anyone who views those proceedings will be struck by the obvious dismay, disappointment and anger that was brought on by the announcement of the application FAR.

But the ASAP recommendation which most threatens to kill the Commercial Crew baby in its crib is the panel's preference for *both* cost-plus contracts *and* FAR. ASAP evidently *truly believes* the SAA route will be more dangerous for crew. As I will show shortly, they even question whether vehicles built under SAA guidelines can be made cheaper than those built under FAR. However, there is evidence to indicate that this attitude has more to do with *the combination of* three things: an unquestioned belief in the second myth stated in Chapter 2, not acquainting themselves with the details of the working manufacturing processes and safety procedures used by the Commercial Crew participants, and possibly not being familiar with all of the relevant NASA studies on the subject. For reasons about to be explained, it appears that the ASAP group is not bothering *to actually examine* the details of what Commercial Crew companies *are doing* in their factories as far as safety and cost reduction are concerned. It seems as though they operate under the naïve notion that NASA *always* knows more than anyone else, so anything not *totally* managed by NASA on the *minutest* level *cannot possibly* be right.

Evidence that ASAP does not believe SAA offers true cost savings over FAR and can be as safe is reflected in the following statement by ASAP Chairman Vice Admiral Joseph W. Dyer, USN (retired) before the Subcommittee on Space and Aeronautics of the House Committee on Science, Space, and Technology. In Admiral Dyers *own words* concerning CCiCap:

> *"The ASAP strongly believes that only a cost[-plus] type contract is appropriate for Phase 2. We believe that fixed price type contracts are appropriate for low risk undertakings where the requirements are clearly understood by both the government and the contractor(s). Phase 2 is neither, and we believe both schedule and safety would be enhanced in a cost-plus environment. Why? While Space Act Agreements (SAAs) may have stimulated new companies to enter the business, much remains unsettled. Design has preceded requirements, and with the recent phased approach, NASA is just now undertaking to determine how systems will be certified to transport NASA astronauts to and from the ISS. This timing increases programmatic risk and has serious potential to impact safety.*
>
> *Additionally, any number of Department of Defense (DOD) programs provides evidence that the presumed cost advantages of fixed price development may be illusory."* (Dyer b 2012)

His argument that cost-plus contracts (together with FAR) necessarily enhance safety whilst fixed-cost SAA contracts *"timing increases programmatic risk and has serious potential to impact safety"* doesn't take a number of factors into account which have already been covered in earlier pages of this book. Also, remember the Space Foundation study which indicates the extensive micro-control in the Shuttle program (in which FAR based cost-plus contracts were implemented) *actually led to the Shuttle being less safe.* (Space Foundation 2012)

If ASAP's suspicion is true that Commercial Crew companies' SAA or non-NASA projects would be prone to be less safe than projects tightly controlled by NASA to the *smallest* detail, how do they explain SpaceX's development procedures? A NASA FAR based cost-plus contract would require any participating company's vehicle to have its structural integrity meet a tolerance of 125% of what is needed to give reasonable safety (according to current published NASA safety standards), but SpaceX *even before becoming part of NASA's Commercial Cargo and Commercial Crew program* have not accepted less than 140% tolerance on the Falcon 9. SpaceX is applying the same requirement to the Falcon Heavy that the company is developing *completely independent of NASA* or any other government agency. (Money a 2012)

Also, SpaceX's Falcon 9 launch vehicle is the first launcher since the Saturn V super rocket of the 1960s capable of *safely* completing an orbital mission with up to 2 first stage engines not working. This feature actually saved astronauts' lives during the Apollo program that sent Americans to the Moon; however, it is not a safety requirement specified by NASA to SpaceX or ULA. *But SpaceX designed Falcon 9 that way anyway in order to add a much greater level of safety and reliability.* If the ASAP claim that the Commercial Crew suppliers will try to cut corners is valid, how do they explain SpaceX *exceeding* the safety specifications that NASA requires of them with no urging to do so from NASA?

ASAP may counter the above argument with the point that just because SpaceX is that conscientious on its own, it doesn't mean another company would be. Of course, that is true. That's why NASA should indeed constantly make sure its safety requirements are met. However, that level of safety regulation *does not require* FAR/cost-plus contracts which could actually *compromise* safety (as the Space Foundation study indicates).

To what particular studies is Admiral Dyer alluding when he says *"any number of Department of Defense (DOD) programs provides evidence that the presumed cost advantages of fixed price development may be illusory"*? What specific evidence in these supposed studies would point in that direction? He doesn't say. What's more, his statement seems to indicate complete lack of knowledge regarding the earlier mentioned Air Force/NASA study, which came to the conclusion the SpaceX Falcon 9 launcher cost many times less than if it had been developed under NASA's traditional way of doing things involving FAR based cost-plus contracts. And that while *exceeding* NASA's published structural safety requirements!

Also, ASAP appears to be concerned about the fact that commercial space flight companies, in offering flights for the commercial market, may operate under a different set of safety rules from the ones NASA will use for vehicles it contracts for flights to ISS. Evidence of that attitude comes from this passage in their report for 2012:

> *"The ASAP is concerned that some will champion an approach that is a current option contained in the Commercial Crew Integrated Capability (CCiCap) agreement. There is risk this optional, orbital flight-test demonstration with a non-NASA crew could yield two standards of safety— one reflecting NASA requirements, and one with a higher risk set of commercial requirements. It also raises questions of who acts as certification authority and what differentiates public from private accountability. Separating the level of safety demanded in the system from the unique and hard-earned knowledge that NASA possesses introduces new risks and unique challenges*

to the normal precepts of public safety and mission responsibility. We are concerned that NASA's CCiCap 2014 "Option" prematurely signals tacit acceptance of this commercial requirements approach absent serious consideration by all the stakeholders on whether this higher level of risk is in fact in concert with national objectives." (Dyer a et al. 2013)

When ASAP says, *"two standards of safety—one reflecting NASA requirements, and one with a higher risk set of commercial requirements"*, what is the basis for asserting the set of commercial requirements would be any more risky than NASA requirements? He doesn't give any data to back up that assumption. Currently, NASA is responsible for the safety requirements in regard to vehicles servicing NASA missions and carrying NASA astronauts, whilst the FAA is responsible for safety requirements of vehicles that would be used for purely commercial passenger trips not related to any government agency. For generations the FAA has shown itself to be diligent in guarding the public's safety through creation and enforcement of effective regulations for passengers carried on flying vehicles. What makes ASAP think that the FAA are going to be any less professional and conscientious than their previous history would suggest in the specific case of orbital spaceflight?

NASA will need their vehicles to be capable of carrying out various types of special missions that commercial passenger spaceflight companies will **never** *do.* The special requirements of such missions may entail extra unique safety features that would give no added measure of safety to the stand-alone commercial industry. Why saddle the commercial industry with extra expensive requirements designed for special types of flights unique to NASA that the private transport companies will never perform? That is the whole reason why the FAA was given jurisdiction over commercial space traffic instead of NASA. Who says the FAA is so much less competent than NASA that this dual regulatory system will mean a *"higher level of risk"*? On the contrary, could the extra NASA-specific safety requirements actually result in situations that would be *less safe* for commercial industry flights if the industry was forced to adopt those requirements? Furthermore, would these extra regulations and associated extra hardware modifications and procedures constitute a serious financial burden on a profit making enterprise? In regard to those two points involving safety and economic efficacy, remember the conclusions of the *Space Foundation* report mentioned earlier in regard to normal NASA safety procedures: NASA's standard operational procedures could make vehicles less safe and excessively expensive!

There is an aviation example I can give you which might help illustrate this point. During the Shuttle program a specially modified Boeing 747 was used to haul the Shuttle great distances across the country by piggybacking it on the plane. NASA had special safety requirements that necessitated hardware modifications to a stock 747 before they could use it to fly a Shuttle from place to place. It also had special vehicle operating standards that needed to be applied to the airplane to insure safe flight operations. *Would it have made sense to make **all** 747's (even the ones carrying commercial passengers) comply with those same NASA hardware and operational rules?* Of course not! Those rules could actually make a commercial airliner both *uneconomical* and *less safe.* No, *the FAA* decides what civilian commercial aircraft safety standards are, not NASA! In the same manner, NASA space missions and space hardware requirements for a SpaceX Dragonrider/Falcon 9 or an Atlas V/Dream Chaser combo may need to be *totally different* from the safety requirements needed for similar vehicles on purely commercial flights. To have NASA enforce *their* spacecraft safety standards *(developed for NASA-specific missions)* on the commercial space industry as a whole for flights *having nothing to do with NASA missions* could be catastrophic, both economically and from a safety standpoint. Thus, *the FAA* has been given the responsibility for *non-NASA* commercial space safety regulations along with the power to enforce those regulations, just as they do for commercial aircraft. It would be wise not to hand that responsibility over to NASA.

It seems as though ASAP is pushing for NASA to be the governing safety body for *both* NASA flights and *unrelated* commercial vehicles by edging the FAA out of the picture. In other words, because *up until now,* only NASA vehicles sent people to orbit and NASA specified the safety regulations for those vehicles, ASAP apparently *assumed* that they should also be in charge of safety requirements for *all* space vehicles from now on. More White Queen thought processes.

The overarching point is, ASAP appears to have the naïve "good intentions" evinced by Mr. Shaw, that could ultimately lead U.S. spaceflight into the infernal nether regions.

Another point along this line is that once the Commercial Crew trips to ISS prove the usefulness and serviceability of commercial vehicles for passenger service, then companies such as Bigelow will begin putting space stations up. There will be so many of these stations that there will soon be *far* more passenger traffic to these stations than on NASA missions. Now the simple fact is that *any* form of transportation will eventually have fatal accidents. Elementary probability principles tell us that if similar vehicles are used and traffic is much greater for purely commercial flights than NASA flights to ISS, then the odds are that accidents will occur more frequently for independent commercial flights than for NASA flights, *even if NASA-operated and industry-operated vehicles are equally safe.* For instance, if for every 50 NASA flights, there are 500 purely commercial flights during the same time period, mathematics dictates the chance of an accident during that time period is 500 divided by 50 or 10 times higher for the purely commercial flights – *even if all of the vehicles are equally safe*! The probability of an accident would go up merely because *many more* purely commercial vehicles would be flying than NASA mission vehicles.

Given the weird "White Queen" logic exhibited by ASAP and space committee politicians, if an industry accident happens before NASA has a Commercial Crew accident of its own, certain politicians and the Old Guard might *possibly* represent it as "proof" the FAA regulated vehicles are less safe and that NASA should be put in charge of promulgating safety regulations. Furthermore, it would not be surprising if it was stated the new regulations should be executed via implementing old-style traditional contracting methods for both the manufacturing and flight of private orbital space vehicles; thereby, giving NASA micro-control of the development and operation of *all* space vehicles produced in America. If such a scenario arises, let's hope the voices of reason can stand up to such knee-jerk emotionalism.

Also, the following irrational claim has been made to me by Commercial Crew opponents. They say that when the first fatal accident of a commercially developed vehicle occurs (whether on a NASA mission or a for-profit passenger flight) there will be such a great outrage from the public that they will *demand* NASA be given back its former role of being the only designer and developer of launchers and orbital space vehicles for human passengers, at which point Commercial Crew will then be killed by acclamation. They point to the outpouring of national grief that occurred after the fatal flights of Challenger and Columbia as evidence of how intense the public reaction would be. But let's analyze the thought processes behind such thinking by doing a relevant comparison with the early days of commercial aviation.

In the early twentieth century, air flight was as dangerous as spaceflight is today. Charles Lindberg was as great a national hero after his flight across the Atlantic as any astronaut ever was. Other famous heroic aviators and public figures who were idolized by the public were no less mourned than astronauts of the current era when they met an untimely end during their flights. The deaths of legendary aviator Wiley Post and beloved comedic actor Will Rogers in a commercially produced airplane come to mind, yet the massed public of that time did not call for an end to commercial air travel.

So currently, orbital spaceflight is as risky as air flight was back then. If people want to take the risk *fully knowing the danger*, why stop it? It's their money and their life. Every year people risk their lives climbing dangerous peaks like Mount Everest and quite often lose their lives in the attempt. Do you hear anybody screaming for the outlawing of mountain climbing every time someone dies in that endeavor?

But even worse is a hidden elitist assumption behind this silly attitude. That the great mass of the public will be more upset that *a few people* meet their untimely demise on a spacecraft than when *300 people* abruptly die in a large airliner crash. This supposition would *imply* the lives of space travelers somehow are considered *more valuable* than the lives of the people who die in air crashes, when any sane person would consider all human life equally precious. Why should we call for the end of commercially designed and developed spacecraft after a fatal accident when we don't do that after aviation fatalities? That blasted White Queen rears her ugly head again!

Ironically, the higher flight rate of purely commercial flights could ultimately make all space vehicles (including NASA's) safer much sooner. Higher flight rates lead to more experienced and competent flight mechanics, lessons learned as to what can go wrong will be discovered sooner and the underlying problems gotten out of the way faster. This methodology gradually leads to less and less going wrong. So even though there may be more civilian accidents *at first*, the rate at which they happen would plummet much faster due to their earlier discovery brought on by the higher flight rate. *This protracted mechanism is how the commercial airline industry ultimately became the safest means of transportation ever devised by humans.* I make this point, not because I am callous about the loss of human life, but merely because in *any* form of transportation some fatalities are inevitable and there is *no way* to totally get rid of them. Tens of thousands of people die in highway accidents in the U.S. every year, but that is not considered to be a reason to stop automobile travel. Instead, the safety features of automobiles are being constantly improved, with the result that the number of deaths on American highways is much lower than it was a few decades ago.

But just because the NASA "Old Guard" faction might attempt to misuse legitimate issues such as safety to stifle our nation's progress in the new commercial space arena (despite the resistance of their more forward-looking colleagues in the agency), let us not forget what has always been good about NASA that more than justifies its continued existence and *makes it a valuable asset.* Indeed, if the negative reactionary influences can be eradicated from the agency and pork politics can be countered whilst giving the NASA employees who are less afraid of change greater reign on the agency's future, *NASA may yet experience a golden age that would make the Apollo era pale by comparison.* In the next chapter we will examine that more positive aspect of our country's space agency.

Chapter 7: NASA as technology incubator *and* cutting edge space explorer

"Governments will always play a part in solving huge problems. … They also fund basic research, which is a crucial component of the innovation that improves the lives of everyone."
-- *Bill Gates*

"Innovation is the process of turning ideas into manufacturable and marketable form."
-- *Watts Humphrey: pioneering software engineer*

Much text in this book has been written to explain the capabilities of the Commercial Crew participants and how they are the key to giving NASA affordable access to space. However, the main reason why those companies are in a position to do what they are doing now is because they have taken technologies originally developed during NASA projects of previous decades and refined those technologies to the point where they are economically practical and potentially profitable for commercial applications.

7.1 The ultimate source of American space technology

For example, not too long ago, NASA developed an extraordinary heat shield material called <u>PICA</u>. SpaceX (with the aid of NASA engineers) has taken this technology and improved it to produce the re-entry heat shield for their Dragonrider spacecraft.

Figure 19: Orion-MPCV (Image credit: NASA)

Reentry speed of vehicles returning from the Moon is 7,000 miles per hour higher than the reentry speed that is experienced by orbital spacecraft such as the Space Shuttle and any of the proposed Commercial Crew spacecraft. The heat shield on the old Apollo command module and also on the Orion-MPCV spacecraft (that Congress is forcing NASA to develop) both are made from a substance called AVCOAT which would allow those spacecraft to survive these much greater reentry speeds and the associated greater heat. (Edwards, Hautaluoma, and Clem 2009) Like Apollo command modules, Orion spacecraft are designed to be flown only once then thrown away.

Contrast that to the heat shield on both the cargo and human transportation versions of the SpaceX Dragon spacecraft which uses a material derived from NASA's PICA. It is made such that it would allow a spacecraft and its occupants to survive a re-entry at the *even higher* speeds, stresses and temperatures associated with the return from distances *far beyond* the Moon in the remote depths of space away from the Earth's gravity well. (Clark b 2010) Furthermore, the Dragon cargo vessel and Dragonrider with their associated shield are *reusable*, unlike the use-once-throw-away Apollo and Orion.

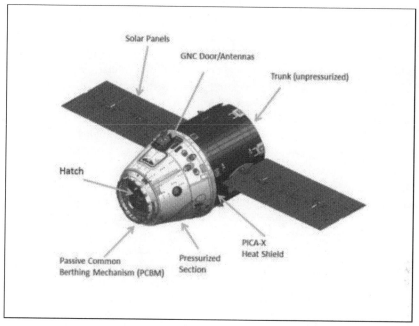

Figure 20: Dragon spacecraft (Image credit: SpaceX)

As mentioned in Chapter 3, Orion is just another vehicle being pushed on NASA at the behest of certain politicians and some upper level agency management in a similar manner to SLS. The difference is that construction of Orion was begun years earlier under project Constellation, had already consumed billions in development money before SLS was even announced, and threatens to consume even more billions before a final spacecraft is produced. Though, unlike SLS, it looks as though working Orion hardware *might* yet see service. It is essentially a souped-up Apollo capsule that is claimed to be for deep space missions when, in reality, such missions would be better served by a *true* spaceship such as the earlier mentioned NAUTILUS-X.

How can we confidently think the SpaceX PICA-derived heat shield material can *actually* withstand an interplanetary reentry? Because NASA's *Stardust* spacecraft that returned comet dust to Earth from interplanetary space had a PICA shield (Tran et al. 1997) and the SpaceX shield is an *improved* version of that.

Like the SpaceX Dragonrider, the Boeing CST-100 will also use a more advanced heat shield material known as the Boeing Lightweight Ablator or BLA. Though I have not been able to find out for sure, it would not surprise me if BLA is also a descendant of PICA, since Boeing developed and manufactured the original PICA for NASA. The CST-100 would also be reusable.

Another example of NASA derived technology is the Dream Chaser reusable space plane that Sierra Nevada Corporation is putting forward as its spacecraft for astronaut transport in the Commercial Crew program. This spacecraft is based on research done with the HL-10 lifting body designed by NASA (built by Northrup) which flew from the late 1960s to the mid-1970s. It was hoped the research would ultimately lead to an orbital vehicle with significant glide capability. The advantage of gliding is it gives a larger cross-range and thus more flexibility by offering a choice from a greater number of landing sites spread over a much larger area than would be possible with a capsule such as Orion, CST-100 or Dragonrider. Indeed, Dream Chaser appears to be the fruition of that goal, with its capability of horizontal glide landings on airport runways similar to the way the Space Shuttle did.

It should be noted the CST-100, Dream Chaser and Dragonrider would all be capable of transporting 7 people at a time: the same occupant capacity as the Space Shuttle. Orion-MPCV could only carry a maximum of 4 for the beyond low Earth orbit missions it is supposed to perform.

Bigelow Aerospace's inflatable space station modules are another example of a technology derived from NASA research. In the 1990's, NASA worked on a technology called *TransHab* (short for *Transit Habitation* module) that they hoped would lead to an inflatable replacement for ISS's *Crew Habitation Module* or *CHM*. That latter module was originally intended to be the primary living quarters for the ISS, but construction of the CHM was cancelled. As mentioned in a previous chapter, the advantage of inflatable modules is that they may be launched in a very compact deflated form, then once in space inflated to their full volume. The TransHab featured very effective meteoroid strike protection, highly efficient thermal insulation, and was extremely resistant to air leaks in general via the special multilayer construction of its walls. Later the TransHab project was cancelled as well.

After acquiring exclusive rights to the TransHab patents, Bigelow improved the design in a number of ways, such as replacing the Kevlar® wall layer with Vectran® (which is much stronger than steel) after the module is inflated. (Little 2008) Another interesting idea from Bigelow is constructing Moon base buildings from their inflatable modules and using them in designs for inflatable spacecraft. It is the latter idea that would be used for the NAUTILUS-X deep space exploration spacecraft.

Figure 21: Dream Chaser space plane (Image credit: Sierra Nevada)

7.2 NASA as explorer and frontier expander

In the case of NAUTILUS, a large doughnut-shaped inflatable module (called a torus) would be spun around to generate an "artificial gravity" environment via centrifugal effect. (Holderman 2011)   Any desired strength of apparent gravitational pull can be gotten by choosing an appropriate spin rate. For instance, turning the torus slowly would produce a light effective gravity like that of the Moon, spinning it faster would reproduce a gravitational pull twice that of the Moon to mimic Mars, turning it even faster would give a passenger the weight he/she would have on the surface of the Earth.

Thus, on a trip to Mars, the human occupants of NAUTILUS could gradually become acclimatized to Mars' surface gravity by having the torus rotate to give Earth's gravity at the beginning of the flight and then gradually slow the rotation over days or weeks until they experience the weight they would have on Mars. Conversely, on their way back to Earth, they could become readjusted to Earth's higher gravity and not have to spend convalescent time as ISS astronauts now have to do when they return to back to Earth's surface.

Because of both the gravity flexibility and radiation protection available on the NAUTILUS, the inner Solar System would be totally open to us. With efficient solar power panels, VASIMR should work very well as far away from the Sun as the Asteroid Belt, whilst trips Sunward to orbit around Venus would be easily accomplished.

Venus is far too hot with its 800 degrees Fahrenheit (500 degrees Celsius) surface temperature, highly corrosive atmosphere and high atmospheric pressure to allow direct human exploration to happen;

therefore, we would have to content ourselves with observations from orbit and maybe automated sample return missions.

With its much heavier solar radiation environment and higher temperatures, trips to Mercury might require some fairly challenging life protecting technology be developed; but it wouldn't be as hard as actually landing on as Venus. Near Mercury's poles there is evidence that there may be reserves of water ice which could allow the setting up of an inhabited station, with crater walls offering effective permanent shielding from the Sun's nearby fury. If this valuable resource is indeed available there, Mercury could become a very important outpost for doing valuable solar research, especially considering the threat to our technological civilization that solar flares pose to Earth-based power grids, surface communication infrastructure and orbiting communication satellites.

Figure 22: Light areas indicate possible water ice at Mercury's poles seen from Messenger spacecraft (Image credit: NASA)

As many preceding examples illustrate, technologies based on NASA inventions have been improved and made commercially viable by various aerospace companies *with the help of NASA personnel.* But that doesn't mean those same companies can't come up with some innovative and groundbreaking ideas totally on their own. This point will be illustrated in the next chapter.

Chapter 8: The way to American supremacy in space

"Once we rid ourselves of traditional thinking we can get on with creating the future."
-- James Bertrand

"There's a way to do it better—find it."
-- Thomas Alva Edison

For reasons already explained herein, the U.S. human spaceflight program has been stuck in low Earth orbit for over 40 years. I also covered how the new commercial spaceflight paradigm can allow us to progress deeper into the Solar System in a way SLS/Orion-MPCV cannot, and sooner to boot. Part of that progress can be obtained by getting rid of the peddling of special interests by influential people to the detriment of the country's advancement in the space frontier. Though that step would offer a significant advantage over the old way of doing things, there is another longstanding ingrained thought process that retards us from not only improving how we access space, but also *accelerating* the rate of improvement both now and far into the future.

8.1 The space industry culture of risk aversion

Some people think the problem is that the older space industry companies lack original ideas; that is, they are missing the "outside of the box" thinking SpaceX has evidenced in improving vehicle development and assembly procedures to the extent that they are able to greatly undercut everyone else on launch prices. That simply is not true. There have been some original and even *inspired* innovative ideas that could yield quantum leaps in spacefaring capability within a very short time frame coming from NASA's traditional contractors of previous decades which will be elucidated upon shortly.

Instead, the main stifling problem plaguing the long-time launch vehicle players can be summed up in three words: *extreme risk aversion*. By

119

this I mean, the large traditional NASA contractors are so used to having *all* of their expenses covered under government cost-plus contracts that they won't even try to actually implement great ideas developed in-house if they have to risk *any* company assets to do so. Of course, concerns that stockholders might balk at an expenditure that won't return a profit within a few quarters may be part of the issue.

If one looks at the airliner manufacturing industry, Boeing risked billions on a long term project to develop the state-of-the-art *787 Dreamliner*. This project experienced delays and cost overruns before the completion of the initial production run. However, it is now apparent (after the actual airplane is finally being produced and sold) that it is going to be a major profitable revenue source for the company for many years to come despite the extra time, cost, and numerous problems encountered after its release. The point? If such a large aerospace corporation can successfully execute a big expensive and *risky* aviation development project and sell their shareholders on it beforehand despite the risk, the same "delayed gratification" philosophy ought to be applied to spaceflight development projects -- given that corporation executives explain the potential for enormous payoff and associated risks to shareholders. But just as in aviation, the idea should be to *minimize* economic risk to the investing company, *not* totally eliminate it the way NASA and the Air Force have traditionally done for its contractors with cost-plus contracts.

Indeed, the U.S. Air Force once tried something *somewhat* similar to NASA's new commercial launch course in the 1990s to spur the development of the currently used Atlas V and Delta IV EELVs. Those two launch vehicles were developed by Lockheed-Martin and Boeing, respectively, before they unified their space launcher divisions to form ULA as a new company. What happened as a consequence of that experiment may account (at least in part) for ULA's administration's reticence to try radically new contractual or technical directions.

The Air Force offered Boeing and Lockheed-Martin $500 million dollars as an incentive to develop new launch vehicles, whilst the companies were to supply the remaining money needed to complete development. It was anticipated that a huge demand for satellite launchers in the civilian sector was about to occur with companies (such as Global Star, Iridium and Teledesic) expected to put up huge fleets of communications satellites for cell phone service via satellite, internet and so on. Boeing and Lockheed-Martin would then recoup their invested money servicing this extra commercial business.

However, the customer satellite companies were commercial failures. As a result, it appeared that unless drastic actions were taken, Boeing would have to shut down the Delta IV project. The solution the Air Force came up with was to have Boeing and Lockheed-Martin merge their satellite launcher divisions into the new United Launch Alliance company. To get the two parent companies to go along with that plan, the Air Force promised a $1 billion annual subsidy in addition to paying for each of its satellite launches. That is the way things stand until this day. Boeing and Lockheed-Martin were the only two American manufacturers of large satellite launchers and, for security reasons alone, the Air Force could not rely on foreign rockets of that size.

With the similar SAA based systems such as Commercial Cargo and Commercial Crew, manufacturers aren't assured success, just as in the initial development of Atlas V and Delta IV. However, that puts them on the same playing field risk-wise as most other types of businesses and any company participating in such a program will need to realize that upfront. But as in any major business venture, the potential rewards can be worth the risk when the anticipated opportunity works out.

Opponents of the Commercial Cargo and Commercial Crew programs like to point to the story of Atlas V and Delta IV as a warning that NASA could be in a similar situation where it would have to end up subsidizing the Commercial Crew companies if they *all* happen not to get enough business to continue. This point completely ignores the fact that SpaceX has a large backlog of launches on its manifest (many of which have been secured with large up-front payments) waiting for the production ramp-up of Falcon 9 and the coming Falcon Heavy. (SpaceX f 2013) In the case of ULA, it already has its *guaranteed* Air Force launch business along with some NASA launches other than Commercial Crew.

Part of the reason SpaceX is getting so much launch business is that the prices they are charging are significantly less than anyone else. Atlas V and Delta IV were not priced low enough to take significant trade from their competition. If those two launchers had had aggressively competitive launch prices, they probably would have done well without the extra subsidy from the Air Force just as SpaceX is doing.

Furthermore, the criticism referred to ignores the implication that if Atlas V and Delta IV had been developed using traditional Air Force/NASA acquisition methods, there probably would have been many more billions spent on their development than was the actual case – as one can see from the Air Force/NASA study of the development of Falcon 9.

Notice also that it took a mere four years to develop Atlas V and Delta IV from ground zero, which is almost unheard of for advanced launcher projects. (Aldrin a 2012) A traditional cost-plus development scheme would lack the sense of urgency to recoup the companies' investments that spurred this speed of development.

Another point to be made concerns the earlier mentioned argument that the type of development and contract methods used for Altas V, Delta IV, Commercial Cargo and Commercial Crew lead to less reliable (and hence less safe) vehicles. Both Atlas V and Delta IV have had excellent reliability records for a decade. As was mentioned earlier, those are the launch vehicles which loft the crucial multi-billion dollar spacecraft on which our military forces rely for the sake of their lives and the security of our country.

8.2 A difference in attitude: new space companies versus old

As an example of risk taking with a potentially high payoff which the long established aerospace companies are reticent to pursue, let's look at the issue of launcher reusability. Only one major orbital launcher manufacturer is currently taking on reusability in a serious way with their own money, and that is SpaceX with their _Grasshopper_ test project. They plan to gradually modify Falcon 9's first and second stage boosters to fly back to their launch site and land for quick turn-around and re-use in order to obtain economies of scale in a similar manner to what commercial airliners do. (SpaceX b 2012)

Figure 23: Grasshopper reusable test vehicle in flight (Image credit: SpaceX)

The engineers at SpaceX have estimated a successful conversion to 100% reusability could lower the per launch cost by as much as a factor of 100! (Simberg 2012) This claim is not as far-fetched as it may sound. Remember propellant is currently a _miniscule_ fraction of the cost of a launch and *most of the expense of each launch is tied up in the launcher hardware:* **tens of millions of dollars of hardware that is now thrown away with every single launch.** Obviously, if *the most expensive parts* are reused over and over again whilst also re-flying fairly frequently, then enormous price reduction is possible. However, once the savings from reusability are attained, then fuel cost *will* become a major component of operating costs. Next we will learn how SpaceX is addressing that last problem as well.

Rand Simberg is an actual aerospace engineer who now writes extensively on space related issues. His prior experience *actually working* on major space-related projects probably makes him one of the most technically astute writers on the subject anywhere. As he states:

> *"Bringing down the cost of rocket launches isn't just about reusability; as Musk's quote suggests, it's also about turnaround time. The original premise of the space shuttle program was that the vehicle would be turned around within days; it ended up being months, which is one of the reasons that it never met its cost goals. ...*
>
> *... One of the other reasons that the shuttle was so expensive was that it had very large wings to give the vehicle a thousand miles of cross-range. The Air Force demanded this feature, which would have allowed the shuttle to return to its launch site after a single orbit, though it was never used. But SpaceX doesn't mandate that cross-range feature. Therefore its craft would have to wait a little bit for the Earth to rotate and bring the landing site around again, but this would make SpaceX missions cheaper because the rockets don't have to carry so much propellant in this stage."* (Simberg 2012)

SpaceX is committed to this course, *no matter what*, despite the expectation of a few spectacular crashes of Grasshopper in the process:

> *"CEO Elon Musk, speaking about the Grasshopper program, said in November 2012: "Over the next few months, we'll gradually increase the altitude and speed ... I do think there probably will be some craters along the way; we'll be very lucky if there are no craters. Vertical landing is an extremely important breakthrough – extreme, rapid reusability.""* (Dodson 2012)

Development whilst fully expecting some failures along the way may seem amazing to some people, but it makes a lot of sense if you think about it. Better to work out the worst bugs with unmanned test vehicles long before you fly people. Evidently, SpaceX's attitude is hardware is expendable, people aren't.

Now contrast the above described SpaceX effort to the last reusability project worked on by a couple of longstanding aerospace companies. This work was done under the U.S. Air Force's *Reusable Booster System* (RBS) project. The participants in this program were: Boeing, Lockheed-Martin and one relative newcomer of much smaller size, Andrews Aerospace.

Figure 24: Scale model prototype test for Reusable Booster System project (Image credit: AFRL)

To make a long story short, the Air Force cancelled the project. With no one to pay them to develop a reusable launch vehicle, all the entrants stopped work on their projects. (Foust c 2012) In the case of Andrews Aerospace, that risk aversion was quite understandable since they didn't have the large positive cash flow and huge resources of Boeing, Lockheed-Martin, or SpaceX. Unlike SpaceX's attitude toward reusability, the potential huge payoff that could stem from having a truly reusable vehicle was not enough of an incentive for the two mainstream companies to take the necessary risk they would bear without the Air Force backing. Evidently, both Boeing and Lockheed-Martin consider aviation to be their truly high value mainline business, with space essentially a sideline they participate in when the cards are stacked in their favor. Again, this attitude seems to be the result of years of them not having to take major risks in the space arena because of government largess. This also explains why Lockheed-Martin is involved as the primary contractor for the Orion-MPCV spacecraft: a perfect example of a totally government financed space project with no financial risk to the company. Because of that fact, Orion-MPCV may possibly be costing *billions* more than it needs to.

Thus, Lockheed-Martin is willing to act as the primary contractor for NASA's Orion spacecraft, but yet not do anything daring (such as seriously tackle reusability on its own). Orion is a perfect example of a totally government financed space project with little or no financial risk to the company done in a way similar to how the company usually has operated in the past with space projects.

If Boeing had had a similar attitude to the one they have toward booster reusability vis-à-vis their radical new airliner, they would have possibly been facing extinction in the near future. They are involved in the Commercial Crew program with their CST-100 spacecraft, but NASA is funding most of their costs. You just don't see them going out on the limb *totally on their own* in the way you see SpaceX with Falcon Heavy and Grasshopper.

Even though (in its latest incarnation) ULA was founded in 2006, I count it as a long standing NASA contractor because it was formed via the unification of the commercial orbital launch vehicle divisions of Boeing and Lockheed-Martin, which have done business for decades with the Department of Defense, NASA, and communication corporations. Some of their engineers of the highest caliber came up with the cutting edge ideas in the ULA depot study I mentioned earlier, but ULA is currently not developing hardware for this purpose. (Zegler, Kutter & Barr 2009) Perhaps *the management* of ULA does not want to pursue the development of such new technology unless it is *largely* financed from the outside in a similar manner to its previous NASA contracts with little or no risk to the company. One might also speculate it could have something to do with the fact that its parent companies, Boeing and Lockheed-Martin, have valuable contracts related to SLS/Orion-MPCV which this new technology could obviate.

Anyway, ULA has ceded most of the commercial launch market to Europe's Arianespace and decided to concentrate on U.S. government defense contracts and NASA contracts that often *legally require* American launchers. Since they were the only U.S. company supplying vehicles for lifting large government payloads in the past and had no competition in this area, it was easier for ULA to have a lucrative income just from government contracts. They did not have to worry about keeping their launch prices as low as other companies' prices to keep this government business and thus had little incentive to *drastically* improve both their price/performance ratio and cost efficiency by implementing *radically* new (but financially risky) production methods and technologies to yield maximum effectiveness for the least amount spent. Essentially, the significant improvement of their launch vehicles over the past decades has been via a conservative slow plodding evolutionary process without *revolutionary* advances in efficiency and cost savings.

To be fair, it should be noted ULA is involved as a currently *unfunded* participant in Commercial Crew. However, participation involves much less risk than it did for SpaceX, because ULA are not developing a whole new launch vehicle from scratch the way SpaceX did. As I described earlier, the Atlas V was *already* a sophisticated launch vehicle *with years of successful flight history* before the first flight of SpaceX's Falcon 9. Due to its already existing refinement and sophistication, the cost of modifications to make the Atlas V safe for humans will be relatively minor in comparison to the potential income reward that could precipitate with operational commercial crew operations: both to the ISS and other possible destinations. Even so, just as with Boeing and Lockheed-Martin, there is still no concerted relatively high risk effort to counter SpaceX's assault on the reusability issue or a totally self-financed heavy-lift vehicle such as Falcon Heavy. Apparently, their current strategy is just to pray to God that SpaceX fails in its quest for orbital launcher reusability.

Let's hope ULA sees the light and gives SpaceX a run for its money (at list with reusability), because otherwise, sticking to the old way of doing things will lead to their extinction. Such a situation would *not* be good for the burgeoning American commercial space industry. The more competition there is, the more pressure there will be for all participants to lower launch prices. *Would SpaceX still try as hard to keep prices as low as possible if they were the only American source for large orbital launchers?* I'd *like* to think they would, but for the sake of my country's best interests I don't want to find out for certain in the future. One thing is for sure, a primary reliance on the government teat that is fostered by the actions of a few elected officials on crucial committees does not help the situation any.

Other differences in attitude are reflected in the development of Orion-MPCV versus the current Commercial Crew spacecraft. The <u>Launch Escape System</u> (<u>LES</u>), which is sometimes termed as the <u>Launch Abort System</u> (<u>LAS</u>) on these vehicles is a prime example.

Orion-MPCV has a more robust version of Project Apollo's LES, it being a powerful solid propellant rocket mounted *above* the crewed spacecraft which would *pull* the spacecraft away from its launcher (this pulling leads to it being called a *tractor* system) in the event of an emergency. It is thrown away in flight after *every* launch. Rather than go the old Apollo tractor direction, all of the Commercial Crew participants have eschewed both solid propellant propulsion and the tractor method for their LES. Instead, they have all gone with liquid propellant *pusher* systems which are essential for one of their primary goals: spacecraft reusability. Their LES systems remain with the spacecraft *through-out the entire flight* and may even be used to aid with landing the spacecraft back on Earth at the end of a successful mission.

This also could mean that during the flight to orbit, Orion may possibly be less safe than the Commercial Crew spacecraft. Why? The Commercial Crew LES systems will allow safe return of the crew at virtually *any point* of the way to orbit. Contrast that to the tractor system used on Orion. The LES tower must be *ejected* from the Orion spacecraft at some point and thus be unavailable thereafter. Also it might pose a danger to the crew in case the LES jettison process malfunctions and there is either an incomplete or unsuccessful separation.

126

Figure 25: Diagram of Orion flight abort with LES (Image credit: NASA)

One of the purported advantages of Orion-MPCV pointed to by its proponents is that its life-support systems will sustain a crew longer than the Commercial Crew spacecraft could; that is, for 21 days. (NASA c 2011) First of all, for deep spaceflights to places like L2, one could cut down the Crew on Dragonrider, CST-100 and Dream Chaser from 7 to 4 (the latter number being the number of crew Orion-MPCV is designed to carry on such a mission) and greatly extend the practical life-support period. However, that would not bring life-support up to 21 days for those spacecraft. But the only thing required to match that time limit would be the development of an enhanced service module to hold the extra life-support equipment along with some extra propulsion and still keep the full complement of 7 crew. This could possibly cost hundreds of millions or even billions less than continued development on Orion-MPCV provided it was done via SAAs.

8.3 Lack of innovation is not just a U.S. problem

It's not just American launch vehicle manufacturers who are feeling SpaceX breathing down their necks. As mentioned before, Europe's Ariane line of launch vehicles grabbed away the lion's share of the large commercial satellite launches from the U.S. many years ago, but after seeing the extremely rapid increase of scheduled future launches on SpaceX's commercial launch manifest with the much lower launch prices they are quoting, Arianespace are starting to sweat. (Cowing d 2012)

According to SpaceX CEO, Elon Musk, Arianespace has reason to be worried. He thinks the flag ship of their rocket fleet *Ariane 5* is just the same-old way of doing things that is going to allow him to eat their lunch. In Mr. Musk's words:

> *"I don't say that with a sense of bravado but there's really no way for that vehicle to compete with Falcon 9 and Falcon Heavy. If I were in the position of Ariane, I would really push for an Ariane 6"* (Amos 2012)

The Russians charge less for launches than Arianespace, and hence less than ULA as well. Part of a crafty strategy which allows them to do this is their implementation of a system known to rocket engineers as a *BDB*: for a short explanation of this concept, refer to its definition in the glossary. However, the Russians charge more for launches than the Chinese, even though the latter's rockets are also technically BDBs with the even lower costs coming from the addition of the cheap labor available in China. (Sieff 2012) Given that the Chinese are expected to have problems meeting SpaceX launch prices (as evidenced in an earlier chapter), it appears the Russians may find themselves in a similar jam as the Europeans in regard to SpaceX.

8.4 The "can-do" attitude of SpaceX

All of the above points lead to two questions: "What innovative methods by SpaceX allow its drastically reduced launch prices and its quick gain of market share?" and "Why do these methods work?" Hopefully, constructive answers to those two questions will allow ULA and others the means of competing with SpaceX head-on. Following is a list of just *a few* of those *many* innovations.

SpaceX manufactures 80% of its vehicle parts, rather than extensively rely on subcontractors as their competition does. This strategy gives them greater quality control during every step of the manufacturing process. Also, each middleman added to the manufacturing process must have a profit that adds to the total cost; thus, SpaceX doing almost everything themselves essentially eliminates that extra expense. (SpaceX c 2012)

The same rocket engine is used in every model of launch vehicle produced by SpaceX. Getting a more powerful vehicle is just a matter of adding more engines to the vehicle. This methodology gives them greater economies of scale.

Rethinking the way things have always been done can help. For instance, the electrical systems of rockets had essentially been done the same way since the 1950s. That is, thick bundles of wires running along the length of the vehicle (held by wiring harnesses) would transmit the sensor and control signals used to monitor the operation of the rocket and control it in flight. Starting with its experimental Falcon 1 launcher, SpaceX replaced many of these much heavier and more complicated bundles of wires with a very thin commonly available Ethernet cable that wired home or office networks use for computer to computer communication. Each Ethernet cable would carry as much data traffic as a whole big bundle of wires did before. (SpaceX d 2008)

The design of the Falcon 9's airframe (support structure and outside walls) is totally different as well. To see the contrast, let's first look at how their competition makes an airframe.

ULA makes its launcher airframes from aluminum plate about two inches thick for strength. However, a solid two inch thick booster wall would result in a rocket that is too heavy to fly. They get around this problem by removing aluminum through boring out a large number of deep pockets in the wall up until the point where there is an almost paper thin layer left on the outside opposite each bore hole. The honeycombing that results from this method gives the wall the strength it needs to withstand the huge differences in internal and outer pressure during flight as well as the enormous stresses to which the vehicle is subjected, with a corresponding *drastic* decrease in weight. However, this procedure is very time consuming, which of course translates into extra labor expense. What's more, most of the original mass of aluminum is cast away from the boring operation, meaning that a company has to pay for much more aluminum than will actually end up being used in the airframe. (Anderson 2a 2012)

One might think it would be better for ULA to manufacture an airframe the way it is done in the airline manufacture industry. The method of manufacture used there is to take thin sheets of metal, bend them into the shape that is needed, and rivet the sheets to ribs and hoops for strength. ULA doesn't do that because rivets *can't handle* the tremendous pressure differential between the inside and outside of the booster without leaking, and thus, severely weakening the airframe. Instead, they resort to the above described bore out method. (Anderson 2a 2012)

SpaceX figured out a technique that allows them to produce airframes in a similar manner to what is done in the airliner manufacturing industry. They use thin sheets of aluminum bent into the proper shape, which then must be held in shape and strengthened by the aforementioned ribs and hoops. They solve the rivet problem *by not using rivets!* Instead they implement a state-of-the-art method called *stir welding*. The metal on each side of the joint to be welded is softened with a custom made machine so that, not only do rivet holes (that would cause leaking) need not be drilled, but the metal does not even have to be melted to make the weld. The resulting structure is stiffer and lighter than ones produced by way of the traditional method and very little of the original mass of aluminum is lost. (Anderson 2a 2012)

The above solutions are just a few of the new radical ideas practically applied at SpaceX. Mr. Musk has publicly stated many times in a large number of venues that SpaceX has many secret processes they are not registering for patent because details would have to be published to obtain the patent and they don't want to give the Chinese a free ride.

8.5 American moxie is not confined to SpaceX

On the surface it appears it is up to ULA and Orbital to step up to the plate with innovation, if our country is to have multiple orbital launcher sources in the future. In fact, the latter of the two is involved in a project that may be up to the task.

Specifically, Microsoft billionaire Paul Allen is a primary backer of *StratoLaunch Systems* (StratoLaunch 2012) which intends to use a large aircraft to lift a multistage rocket and payload to a high altitude, then have the rocket propel the satellite or manned spacecraft into orbit. The companies involved in this enterprise are Scaled Composites (aircraft), Orbital Sciences (rocket) and Dynetics (mating and integration with payload). With such a prominent well-known investor and major aerospace corporations involved, this would seem more than just another want-to-be "vaporware" organization.

Furthermore, it is the intention of Virgin Galactic, XCOR and Blue Origin to eventually expand from their initial suborbital space tourist operations to the launching of orbital satellites and passenger spacecraft.

So it appears the future of American spaceflight is bright indeed, but it could be greatly accelerated and become an even greater economic advantage to our nation if more of the funds NASA receives could *actually* be used to accomplish its stated goals. Now is the time for our citizens to insist our politicians abstain from actions that inhibit our progress.

Chapter 9: It's up to *us*!

"Someone once said that every form of government has one characteristic peculiar to it and if that characteristic is lost, the government will fall. In a monarchy, it is affection and respect for the royal family. If that is lost the monarch is lost. In a dictatorship, it is fear. If the people stop fearing the dictator, he'll lose power. In a representative government such as ours, it is virtue. If virtue goes, the government fails. Are we choosing paths that are politically expedient and morally questionable? Are we in truth losing our virtue? . . . If so, we may be nearer the dustbin of history than we realize."
    -- *Ronald Reagan*

"That which can be destroyed by the truth should be."
    -- *P.C. Hodgell*

"If the dinosaurs had had a space program, they'd still be here."
    -- *Rick Tumlinson: cofounder of the Space Frontier Foundation* speaking at
    the inauguration of *Deep Space Industries, Inc.*

A virtue which is truly essential for survival of our form of government is to have elected officials who will (at least *occasionally*) give precedence to doing what is best for the *entire* country in the long term *rather than* always working for the temporary gain of only *certain parts* of society. With this idea in mind, I hope this book will accomplish its primary objective: to alert enough caring American citizens and politicians about actions that are either intentionally or unintentionally having a negative effect on our nation's spaceflight capability. We should eliminate those things which are essentially in Ms. Hodgell's words, *"That which can be destroyed by the truth"*. Perhaps enough voices raised in righteous indignation will put an end to some of the short-sighted pursuit of *transient regional* advantages with little concern for what is the best outcome for the Republic as a whole.

I remember during the 2008 U.S. Presidential campaign there was a lot of public discussion and consternation over the waste of money on what was called "The Bridge to Nowhere" in Alaska. People all over the country were outraged that $233 million of Federal money was being wasted on a bridge in an area where it would see very little traffic and serve few people.

The project was eventually cancelled. This leads me to believe that if the truth about SLS could get enough publicity, then maybe the majority of politicians outside of the regular space states would do something about this albatross around NASA's neck. After all, the amount of funds thrown away on the <u>RTN</u> outstrips the Alaska boondoggle by orders of magnitude!

So I ask my readers, tell your elected representatives about what you learned in the pages of this book. Inform your fellow citizens and media professionals. Only then can we stand a chance of taking our space program out of the hands of special interests that are gradually destroying it through inaccurate preconceptions, greed or both. Only then will we be able to have the leadership in space that will give our country the technological, scientific and industrial edge it needs for a bright future. We will do it not with primarily government centered spaceflight, and *perhaps* not through only private industry by itself, but via a much faster and economical synergistic partnership between the public and private sectors. It goes back to the concept of *gestalt*: the whole is greater than the sum of the parts. Each one of these segments going it alone and separately will not make as much real progress. *Real progress* is indeed needed, because make no mistake about it, space will be a crucial *make or break* area of international competition for this century and ever after.

If it is left up to the new space innovators, such real progress will occur whether NASA participates or not. As Mr. Musk has often stated, he created SpaceX because he wants humanity to spread to Mars, not only to make money, though he knows making money is essential if SpaceX is going exist long enough to reach his goal. *However, a partnership with NASA that includes SpaceX, ULA, and others could allow America to begin reaping the technological and economic windfall* **much sooner.**

The cancelling of SLS (optimally along with Orion-MPCV) by itself will not be enough for NASA to continue to be of benefit to the American people. One thing that will absolutely be a necessity is for there to be some distancing of Congress from actual NASA operations. *It should be left up to the engineers and scientists at NASA as to what technologies are best to tackle specific programs.* The Executive Branch of the government typically proposes the *general* direction and goals of the agency based on recommendations from qualified scientists and engineers. Congress has traditionally decided which of the proposals are worthy of funding and by how much, but members of Congress **should not** be making engineering decisions on what technologies are to be used to implement specific projects. They don't have the training for that, and the wasting of enormous amounts of national treasury is *inevitable* when they do.

One important question is, "How can the necessary distance be kept between NASA and the special interests served by some politicians?" Honestly, I for one do not have the political acumen and experience to suggest an effective mechanism for permanently accomplishing this end. I hope there are enough dedicated people whose talent is in that line of work and who will adequately tackle the problem.

An equally pressing question is, "What mechanisms can be used to winnow out mentally inflexible executives in the upper and middle levels of NASA (who insist on following old obsolete practices) *without going too far* and throwing out the large number of valuable personnel and already existing methodologies that *still* offer an advantage to the agency?" This is the old conundrum of how to "separate the wheat from the chaff". Coming up with a way to walk such a delicate line will not be easy. Again, finding a way to do so would require persons more politically astute than I.

One thing is certain, if the immediately preceding two issues are not adequately addressed, we will eventually be faced with another abuse of NASA that could possibly be even greater than SLS. Another such ineffective self-serving project could very well signal the death knell of the agency. America would then be faced with an outcome that would leave the burgeoning commercial space industry without an outside source to develop the needed new technologies and exploratory missions that *initially* would not be profitable.

The *majority* of us *expect* that *our* space program (that we paid for with *our* tax dollars) should *not* be thought of *mainly* as a jobs program for make-work projects with no *real* quantified purpose. It is mandatory we have a *truly forward advancing* endeavor which emphasizes the creation of *new* scientific and technological advances that are needed to enable daringly *innovative* spaceflight, and in so doing, generate high paying and long term jobs nationwide. Not something like SLS which (as cited earlier by the former Executive Secretary of the National Space Council during the G.H.W. Bush administration) is, *"too expensive, too slow, and too old."* (Foust a 2012) *As the evidence brought to light in this book indicates, if people had* **purposely** *set out to design a project* **to inhibit** *American progress in space exploration, one could hardly come up with a more effective way of doing so than SLS.* The addition of Orion-MPCV does not make the situation any better either.

Applying the same *outmoded* methods and *obsolete* technologies used in past decades is a *surefire* recipe for failure in twenty-first century spacefaring. Instead, NASA needs an alternative paradigm that is *truly worthy* of its vast pool of scientific and engineering talent. As the same notable personage mentioned above stated, if we choose modern methods over the old bureaucratically entrenched methodology, then at current NASA budget levels "… *we could have an absolutely unbelievable space program."* (Foust a 2012)

The main difficulty we have is that there are certain key politicians and their supporters who like SLS/Orion-MPCV because doing things in the most expensive and man-hour intensive way is **an attractive feature** *to them, rather than a* **problem**. As long as they think NASA is primarily a make-work jobs program for their local constituencies and they also have the wherewithal to tinker with

133

NASA to such an extent that they can essentially *treat it* as such a program, our status as a major space power in the twenty-first century is in jeopardy.

One piece of recent news should stand as a wakeup call that investing in true space travel progress may not be a luxury, but a necessity to protect our populace. The small asteroid that exploded over Russia in February 2013 was closer to being a catastrophe than many people realize. Refined calculations of its energy release concluded that its explosive yield was around or somewhat less than 440 kilotons of TNT – about 30 times the power of the atomic bomb detonated over Hiroshima! (Fountain 2013) Only this *very small* asteroid's extremely high altitude and angle of trajectory at detonation averted the tens of thousands of deaths that would have occurred if it had exploded at a much lower height or steeper path angle.

Now consider, the largest explosion in modern history occurred over (fortunately sparsely populated) Tunguska, Siberia, Russia in 1908 with an explosive yield that leveled trees for 830 square miles! That detonation of a somewhat larger small asteroid has been estimated to have had many times the strength of the 2013 explosion at 3 to 10 megatons (Singer 2007) and was instigated at a low enough altitude to give out extremely extensive damage. Imagine what would happen if such an event happened over even a moderately populated area. Further, think about the fact that we astrophysicists estimate that only a small percentage of asteroids whose paths cross Earth's orbit are known to us.

It's just a matter of time before one of these space travelling boulders explodes low enough over a populated area and brings about an enormous death toll.

Finally, there is the event to which Mr. Tumlinson alluded. An asteroid several miles wide served as the coup de grace for the dinosaurs. There could be such a huge rock with humanity's name on it, and a thriving space program (that is capable of altering such a body's trajectory to render it harmless) could prove to be of truly *vital* importance. These extremely large bodies are much rarer than either of the rocks that caused the incidents in 1908 and 2013, *but that potential is still there* and always will be.

It is clear we need some kind of planetary defense system to detect both the more numerous relatively small asteroids and the less prevalent huge dinosaur killers. These objects need to be spotted long before they reach Earth in order for steps to be taken which can alter their courses into harmless paths. The sooner they are spotted, the easier it is to nudge them into a safe orbit. We can also turn such a system to our economic advantage for our operations in space because some of these objects may be sources of valuable in-space resources that would not have to be expensively hauled up into space from Earth's surface through our planet's money eating gravity well. Such a system is tailor made for an extensive partnership between an *efficiently* organized NASA and private industry.

But a thriving commercial space industry will offer *more immediate* down-to-Earth economic advantages than mining asteroids. As mentioned before, such an extensively active industry *with high flight rates* will also serve as a needed major *long-term* economic stimulus and help spur forward the scientific and technical advancement that will help keep America a rich and prosperous nation well into the future. But this bright future will happen *only* if we take up the challenge to break out of some very bad habits we have developed in the last few decades.

What it boils down to is that there are some people who need to care more about their country's future in space and let loose of their excessive loyalty to the old way of doing things. This would actually help insure NASA's survival rather than making it increasingly impotent from working on a vehicle that will not advance its goals. I and others are tired of politicians and a few old-style NASA executives imposing impractical projects on the talented people at NASA when it is the latter who unfairly get the blame for the subsequent failure.

It is time for the narrow parochial interests with too much power and influence to stop setting NASA up for failure. If things keep going the way they have been up until now, it is a certainty that the *true* enemies of NASA will have all the ammunition they need to abolish the agency. There will be no one to blame but people whose interests lie behind the status quo, but even if NASA's demise happens, they will deny it was their fault and may *especially* deny it to themselves.

Having people work on a rocket built with mostly obsolete technology and outdated methods (mandated from outside of the agency) ultimately is a disservice to the people working on it. Making them continue using old methods and technologies on such a project means that when the project is gone, the workers will not have up-to-date skills they can use on a project which uses modern methods and hardware. The politicians need to decide if they want their constituents to have mere make-work for just a few years with no tangible end result (leaving them unemployable in the long run) or help those constituents bite the bullet in the short-run to learn the new skills and technologies which will keep them employed long enough to raise their children to adulthood.

The optimal goal of needed change and mighty accomplishments need not be an exercise in futility. As I have pointed out repeatedly throughout this book, we won't even need to drastically raise NASA's budget in the way many special-interest alarmists urge.

Outstanding scientists and engineers from the Apollo era such as Buzz Aldrin, Chris Kraft and Tom Moser show us they have a thing or two to teach the rest of us in regard to the needed changes that must take place for NASA to surpass its greatest past achievements in the Twenty-First Century. Furthermore, when one looks at the new innovative work of such people as Dr. Alan Wilhite with his associates at Georgia Tech, the outside-of-the-box thinking of great engineers like ULA's Zegler, Kutter and Barr and the daring do of Elon Musk with his colleagues at SpaceX, then all I can say is "Look out world, here comes American spaceflight!"

Now imagine a future where NASA is revitalized *far beyond* its former Apollo glory by the removal of the politically imposed parasitic projects that have been crippling it. A vigorous vibrant institution leading America's vanguard with exciting voyages to Mars and other Inner Solar System destinations using game changing technology such as is envisioned in NAUTILUS-X. Lighting the way along which American industry will follow close upon its heels.

The ancient Roman philosopher Cicero's famous assertion was ever present with me while I wrote this book: "Dum spiro, spero" meaning "While I breath, I hope". But hoping by itself is not enough. We must act decisively to make a positively transformative future possible. The *entire Universe* awaits us in all of its glorious vastness and *boundless* potential, if we aggressively pursue the steps needed to adequately meet the challenge. Let's take the spirit of the state motto of Kansas as the inspiration for our nation's future greatness in spaceflight: "Ad astra per aspera" . . .

. . . *"To the stars through difficulties."*

H.R.1702: The Commercial Space Act of 1998

One Hundred Fifth Congress of the
United States of America
AT THE SECOND SESSION
*Begun and held at the City of Washington on Tuesday,
the twenty-seventh day of January, one thousand nine hundred and
ninety-eight*

An Act

**To encourage the development of a commercial space industry in
the United States, and for other purposes.**

*Be it enacted by the Senate and House of Representatives of the
United States of America in Congress assembled,*

SECTION 1. SHORT TITLE; TABLE OF CONTENTS.

(a)   SHORT TITLE.—This Act may be
cited as the "Commercial Space Act of 1998".

(b)   TABLE OF CONTENTS.—

Sec. 1. Short
title; table of
contents.
Sec. 2.
Definitions.

TITLE I—PROMOTION OF COMMERCIAL
SPACE OPPORTUNITIES

Sec. 101. Commercialization of Space Station.
Sec. 102. Commercial space launch amendments.
Sec. 103. Launch voucher demonstration program.
Sec. 104. Promotion of United States Global Positioning
System standards.
Sec. 105. Acquisition of space science data.
Sec. 106. Administration of
Commercial Space Centers.
Sec. 107. Sources of Earth
science data.

TITLE II—FEDERAL ACQUISITION OF SPACE
TRANSPORTATION SERVICES

Sec. 201. Requirement to procure commercial space transportation services.
Sec. 202. Acquisition of commercial space transportation services.
Sec. 203. Launch Services Purchase Act of 1990 amendments.
Sec. 204. Shuttle privatization.
Sec. 205. Use of excess intercontinental ballistic missiles. Sec. 206. National launch capability study.

SEC. 2. DEFINITIONS.

For purposes of this Act—

(1) the term "Administrator" means the Administrator of the National Aeronautics and Space Administration;

(2) the term "commercial provider" means any person providing space transportation services or other space-related activities, primary control of which is held by persons other than Federal, State, local, and foreign governments;

(3) the term "payload" means anything that a person undertakes to transport to, from, or within outer space, or in suborbital trajectory, by means of a space transportation vehicle, but does not include the space transportation vehicle itself except for its components which are specifically designed or adapted for that payload;

(4) the term "space-related activities" includes research and development, manufacturing, processing, service, and other associated and support activities;

(5) the term "space transportation services" means the preparation of a space transportation vehicle and its payloads for transportation to, from, or within outer space, or in suborbital trajectory, and the conduct of transporting a payload to, from, or within outer space, or in suborbital trajectory;

(6) the term "space transportation vehicle" means any vehicle constructed for the

purpose of operating in, or transporting a payload to, from, or within, outer space, or in suborbital trajectory, and includes any component of such vehicle not specifically designed or adapted for a payload;

(7) the term "State" means each of the several States of the Union, the District of Columbia, the Commonwealth of Puerto Rico, the Virgin Islands, Guam, American Samoa, the Commonwealth of the Northern Mariana Islands, and any other commonwealth, territory, or possession of the United States; and

(8) the term "United States commercial provider" means a commercial provider, organized under the laws of the United States or of a State, which is—

(A) more than 50 percent owned by United States nationals; or

(B) a subsidiary of a foreign company and the Secretary of Transportation finds that—

(i) such subsidiary has in the past evidenced a substantial commitment to the United States market through—

(I) investments in the United States in long term research, development, and manufacturing (including the manufacture of major components and subassemblies); and

(II) significant contributions to employment in the United States; and

(ii) the country or countries in which such foreign company is incorporated or organized, and, if appropriate, in which it principally conducts its business, affords reciprocal treatment to companies described in subparagraph (A) comparable to that afforded to such foreign company's subsidiary in the United States, as evidenced by—

(I) providing comparable opportunities for companies described in subparagraph (A) to participate in Government sponsored research and development similar to that authorized under this Act;

(II) providing no barriers, to companies described in subparagraph (A) with respect to local investment opportunities, that are not provided to foreign companies in the United States; and

(III) providing adequate and effective protection for the intellectual property rights of companies described in subparagraph (A).

TITLE I—PROMOTION OF COMMERCIAL SPACE OPPORTUNITIES

SEC. 101. COMMERCIALIZATION OF SPACE STATION.

(a)POLICY.—The Congress declares that a priority goal of constructing the International Space Station is the economic development of Earth orbital space. The Congress further declares that free and competitive markets create the most efficient conditions for promoting economic development, and should therefore govern the economic development of Earth orbital space. The Congress further declares that the use of free market principles in operating, servicing, allocating the use of, and adding capabilities to the Space Station, and the resulting fullest possible engagement of commercial providers and participation of commercial users, will reduce Space Station operational costs for all partners and the Federal Government's share of the United States burden to fund operations.

(b)   REPORTS.—(1) The Administrator shall deliver to the Committee on Science of the House of Representatives and the Committee on Commerce, Science, and Transportation of the Senate, within 90 days after the date of the enactment of this Act, a study that identifies and examines—

(A)   the opportunities for commercial providers to play a role in International Space Station activities, including operation, use, servicing, and augmentation;

(B)   the potential cost savings to be derived from commercial providers playing a role in each of these activities;

(C)   which   of   the   opportunities described   in   subparagraph   (A)   the Administrator plans to make available to commercial providers in fiscal years 1999 and 2000;

(D)   the specific policies and initiatives the Administrator is advancing to encourage and facilitate these commercial opportunities; and

(E)   the   revenues   and   cost reimbursements to the Federal Government from commercial users of the Space Station.

(2)   The Administrator shall deliver to the Committee on Science of the House of Representatives and the Committee on Commerce, Science, and Transportation of the Senate, within 180 days after the date of the enactment of this Act, an independently conducted market study that examines and evaluates potential industry interest in providing commercial goods and services for the operation, servicing, and augmentation of the International Space Station, and in the commercial use of the International Space Station. This study shall also include updates to the cost savings and revenue estimates made in the study described in paragraph (1) based on the external market assessment.

(3)   The Administrator shall deliver to the Congress, no later than the submission of the

President's annual budget request for fiscal year 2000, a report detailing how many proposals (whether solicited or not) the National Aeronautics and Space Administration received during calendar years 1997 and 1998 regarding commercial operation, servicing, utilization, or augmentation of the International Space Station, broken down by each of these four categories, and specifying how many agreements the National Aeronautics and Space Administration has entered into in response to these proposals, also broken down by these four categories.

(4)   Each of the studies and reports required by paragraphs (1), (2), and (3) shall include consideration of the potential role of State governments as brokers in promoting commercial participation in the International Space Station program.

SEC. 102. COMMERCIAL SPACE LAUNCH AMENDMENTS.

(a) AMENDMENTS.—Chapter 701 of title 49, United States Code, is amended—

(1) in the table of sections—

(A)   by amending the item relating to section 70104 to read as follows:

"70104. Restrictions on launches, operations, and reentries.";

(B)   by amending the item relating to section 70108 to read as follows:

"70108. Prohibition, suspension, and end of launches, operation of launch sites and reentry sites, and reentries.";

(C)   by amending the item relating to section 70109 to read as follows:

"70109. Preemption of scheduled launches or reentries."; and

(D)   by adding at the end the following new items:

"70120. Regulations.

"70121. Report to Congress.".

(2) in section 70101—

(A) by inserting "microgravity research," after "information services," in subsection (a)(3);

(B) by inserting ", reentry," after "launching" both places it appears in subsection (a)(4);

(C) by inserting ", reentry vehicles," after "launch vehicles" in subsection (a)(5);

(D) by inserting "and reentry services" after "launch services" in subsection (a)(6);

(E) by inserting ", reentries," after "launches" both places it appears in subsection (a)(7);

(F) by inserting ", reentry sites," after "launch sites" in subsection (a)(8);

(G) by inserting "and reentry services" after "launch services" in subsection (a)(8);

(H) by inserting "reentry sites," after "launch sites," in subsection (a)(9);

(I) by inserting "and reentry site" after "launch site" in subsection (a)(9);

(J) by inserting ", reentry vehicles," after "launch vehicles" in subsection (b)(2);

(K) by striking "launch" in subsection (b)(2)(A);

(L) by inserting "and reentry" after "conduct of commercial launch" in subsection (b)(3);

(M) by striking "launch" after "and transfer commercial" in subsection (b)(3); and

(N) by inserting "and development of reentry sites," after "launch-site support facilities," in subsection (b)(4);

(3) in section 70102—

(A) in paragraph (3)—

(i) by striking "and any payload" and inserting in lieu thereof "or reentry vehicle and any payload from Earth";

(ii) by striking the period at the end of subparagraph (C) and inserting in lieu thereof a comma; and

143

(iii) by adding after subparagraph (C) the following:

"including activities involved in the preparation of a launch vehicle or payload for launch, when those activities take place at a launch site in the United States.";

(B) by inserting "or reentry vehicle" after "means of a launch vehicle" in paragraph (8);

(C) by redesignating paragraphs (10), (11), and (12) as paragraphs (14), (15), and (16), respectively;

(D) by inserting after paragraph (9) the following new paragraphs:

"(10) 'reenter' and 'reentry' mean to return or attempt to return, purposefully, a reentry vehicle and its payload, if any, from Earth orbit or from outer space to Earth.

"(11) 'reentry services' means—

"(A) activities involved in the preparation of a reentry vehicle and its payload, if any, for reentry; and "(B) the conduct of a reentry.

"(12) 'reentry site' means the location on Earth to which a reentry vehicle is intended to return (as defined in a license the Secretary issues or transfers under this chapter).

"(13) 'reentry vehicle' means a vehicle designed to return from Earth orbit or outer space to Earth, or a reusable launch vehicle designed to return from Earth orbit or outer space to Earth, substantially intact."; and

(E) by inserting "or reentry services" after "launch services" each place it appears in paragraph (15), as so redesignated by subparagraph (C) of this paragraph;

(4) in section 70103(b)—

(A) by inserting "AND REENTRIES" after "LAUNCHES" in the subsection heading;

(B) by inserting "and reentries" after "commercial space launches" in paragraph (1); and

(C)   by inserting "and reentry" after "space launch" in paragraph (2); (5) in section 70104—

(A) by amending the section designation and heading to read as follows:

"§70104.   Restrictions   on   launches, operations,   and reentries";

(B)   by inserting "or reentry site, or to reenter a reentry vehicle," after "operate a launch site" each place it appears in subsection (a);

(C)   by inserting "or reentry" after "launch or operation" in subsection (a)(3) and (4);

(D)   in subsection (b)—

(i)   by striking "launch license" and inserting in lieu thereof "license";

(ii)   by inserting "or reenter" after "may launch"; and

(iii)   by inserting "or reentering" after "related to launching"; and (E) in subsection (c)—

(i)

By amending the subsection heading to read as follows:

"PREVENTINGLAUNCHESANDREENTRIES.—";

(ii)   by inserting "or reentry" after "prevent the launch"; and

(iii)   by inserting "or reentry" after "decides the launch";

(6) in section 70105—

(A)   by inserting "(1)" before "A person may apply" in subsection (a);

(B)   by striking "receiving an application" both places it appears in subsection (a) and inserting in lieu thereof "accepting an application in accordance with criteria established pursuant to subsection (b)(2)(D)";

(C)   by adding at the end of subsection (a) the following: "The Secretary shall transmit to the Committee on Science of the House of Representatives and the Committee on Commerce, Science, and Transportation of the Senate a written notice not later than 30 days after any occurrence when a license is not issued within the deadline established by this subsection.

"(2) In carrying out paragraph (1), the Secretary may establish procedures for safety approvals of launch vehicles, reentry vehicles, safety systems, processes, services, or personnel that may be used in conducting licensed commercial space launch or reentry activities.";

    (D) by inserting "or a reentry site, or the reentry of a reentry vehicle," after "operation of a launch site" in subsection (b)(1);

    (E) by striking "or operation" and inserting in lieu thereof ", operation, or reentry" in subsection (b)(2)(A); (F) by striking "and" at the end of subsection (b)(2)(B);

    (G) by striking the period at the end of subsection (b)(2)(C) and inserting in lieu thereof "; and";

    (H) by adding at the end of subsection (b)(2) the following new subparagraph:

"(D) regulations establishing criteria for accepting or rejecting an application for a license under this chapter within 60 days after receipt of such application."; and

    (I) by inserting ", including the requirement to obtain a license," after "waive a requirement" in subsection (b)(3);

    (J) (7) in section 70106(a)—

    (A) by inserting "or reentry site" after "observer at a launch site";

    (B) by inserting "or reentry vehicle" after "assemble a launch vehicle"; and

    (C) by inserting "or reentry vehicle" after "with a launch vehicle"; (8) in section 70108—

(A) by amending the section designation and heading to read as follows:

"§70108. Prohibition, suspension, and end of launches, operation of launch sites and reentry sites, and reentries"; and

(B) in subsection (a)—

(i)   by inserting "or reentry site, or reentry of a reentry vehicle," after "operation of a launch site"; and

(ii)   by inserting "or reentry" after "launch or operation";

(9) in section 70109—

(A) by amending the section designation and heading to read as follows:

"§70109. Preemption of scheduled launches or reentries";

(B) in subsection (a)—

(i)   by inserting "or reentry" after "ensure that a launch";

(ii)   by inserting ", reentry site," after "United States Government launch site";

(iii)   by inserting "or reentry date commitment" after "launch date commitment";

(iv)   by inserting "or reentry" after "obtained for a launch";

(v)   by inserting ", reentry site," after "access to a launch site";

(vi)   by inserting ", or services related to a reentry," after "amount for launch services"; and

(vii)   by inserting "or reentry" after "the scheduled launch"; and

(C) in subsection (c), by inserting "or reentry" after "prompt launching";

(10) in section 70110—

(A)   by inserting "or reentry" after "prevent the launch" in subsection (a)(2); and

(B)   by inserting "or reentry site, or reentry of a reentry vehicle," after "operation of a launch site" in subsection (a)(3)(B);

(11) in section 70111—

147

(A)   by inserting "or reentry" after "launch" in subsection (a)(1)(A);

(B)   by inserting "and reentry services" after "launch services" in subsection (a)(1)(B);

(C)   by inserting "or reentry services" after "or launch services" in subsection (a)(2);

(D)   by striking "source." in subsection (a)(2) and inserting "source, whether such source is located on or off a Federal range.";

(E)   by inserting "or reentry" after "commercial launch" both places it appears in subsection (b)(1);

(F)   by inserting "or reentry services" after "launch services" in subsection (b)(2)(C);

(G)   by inserting after subsection (b)(2) the following new paragraph:

"(3) The Secretary shall ensure the establishment of uniform guidelines for, and consistent implementation of, this section by all Federal agencies.";

(H)   by striking "or its payload for launch" in subsection(d) and inserting in lieu thereof "or reentry vehicle, or the payload of either, for launch or reentry"; and

(I)   by inserting ", reentry vehicle," after "manufacturer of the launch vehicle" in subsection (d);

(12) in section 70112—

(A)   in subsection (a)(1), by inserting "launch or reentry" after "(1) When a";

(B)   by inserting "or reentry" after "one launch" in subsection (a)(3);

(C)   by inserting "or reentry services" after "launch services" in subsection (a)(4);

(D)   in subsection (b)(1), by inserting "launch or reentry" after "(1) A";

(E)   by inserting "or reentry services" after "launch services" each place it appears in subsection (b);

148

(F)　　　by inserting "applicable" after "carried out under the" in paragraphs (1) and (2) of subsection (b);

(G)　　by　　inserting　　"OR REENTRIES" after "LAUNCHES" in the heading for subsection (e);

(H)　　　by inserting "or reentry site or a reentry" after "launch site" in subsection (e); and

(I)　　　in subsection (f), by inserting "launch or reentry" after "carried out under a";

(13) in section 70113(a)(1) and (d)(1) and (2), by inserting
"or reentry" after "one launch" each place it appears;

(14) in section 70115(b)(1)(D)(i)—

(A)　　　by inserting "reentry site," after "launch site,"; and

(B)　　　by inserting "or reentry vehicle" after "launch vehicle" both places it appears;

(15) in section 70117—

(A)　　　by inserting "or reentry site, or to reenter a reentry vehicle" after "operate a launch site" in subsection (a);

(B)　　　by inserting "or reentry" after "approval of a space launch" in subsection (d);

(C)　　　by amending subsection (f) to read as follows: "(f) LAUNCH NOT AN EXPORT; REENTRY NOT AN IMPORT.— A launch vehicle, reentry vehicle, or payload that is launched or reentered is not, because of the launch or reentry, an export or import, respectively, for purposes of a law controlling exports or imports, except that payloads launched pursuant to foreign trade zone procedures as provided for under the Foreign Trade Zones Act (19 U.S.C. 81a–81u) shall be considered exports with regard to customs entry."; and

(D)　　　in subsection (g)—

(i)　by striking "operation of a launch vehicle or launch site," in paragraph (1) and inserting in lieu thereof "reentry, operation of a launch vehicle or reentry vehicle, operation of a launch site or reentry site,"; and

    (ii) by inserting "reentry," after "launch," in paragraph (2); and

(16) by adding at the end the following new sections:

"§70120. Regulations

"(a) IN GENERAL.—The Secretary of Transportation, within 9 months after the date of the enactment of this section, shall issue regulations to carry out this chapter that include—

    "(1) guidelines for industry and State governments to obtain sufficient insurance coverage for potential damages to third parties;

    "(2) procedures for requesting and obtaining licenses to launch a commercial launch vehicle;

    "(3) procedures for requesting and obtaining operator licenses for launch;

    "(4) procedures for requesting and obtaining launch site operator licenses; and

    "(5) procedures for the application of government indemnification.

"(b) REENTRY.—The Secretary of Transportation, within 6 months after the date of the enactment of this section, shall issue a notice of proposed rulemaking to carry out this chapter that includes—

    "(1) procedures for requesting and obtaining licenses to reenter a reentry vehicle;

    "(2) procedures for requesting and obtaining operator licenses for reentry; and

    "(3) procedures for requesting and obtaining reentry site operator licenses.

"§70121. Report to Congress

"The Secretary of Transportation shall submit to Congress an annual report to accompany the President's budget request that—

    "(1) describes all activities undertaken under this chapter, including a description of the process for the application for and approval of licenses under this chapter and recommendations for legislation that may further commercial launches and reentries; and

"(2) reviews the performance of the regulatory activities and the effectiveness of the Office of Commercial Space Transportation.".

(b) AUTHORIZATION OF APPROPRIATIONS.—Section 70119 of title 49, United States Code, is amended to read as follows:

"§70119. Authorization of appropriations

"There are authorized to be appropriated to the Secretary of Transportation for the activities of the Office of the Associate Administrator for Commercial Space Transportation—

"(1) $6,275,000 for the fiscal year ending September 30, 1999; and

"(2) $6,600,000 for the fiscal year ending September 30, 2000.".

(c) EFFECTIVE DATE.—The amendments made by subsection

(a)(6)(B) shall take effect upon the effective date of final regulations issued pursuant to section 70105(b)(2)(D) of title 49, United States Code, as added by subsection (a)(6)(H).

SEC. 103. LAUNCH VOUCHER DEMONSTRATION PROGRAM.

Section 504 of the National Aeronautics and Space Administration Authorization Act, Fiscal Year 1993 (15 U.S.C. 5803) is

amended—

(1) in subsection (a)—

(A)   by striking "the Office of Commercial Programs within"; and

(B)   by striking "Such program shall not be effective after September 30, 1995.";

(2) by striking subsection (c); and

(3) by redesignating subsections (d) and (e) as subsections (c) and (d), respectively.

SEC. 104. PROMOTION OF UNITED STATES GLOBAL POSITIONING SYSTEM STANDARDS.

(a)FINDING.—The Congress finds that the Global Positioning System, including satellites, signal equipment, ground stations, data links, and associated command and control facilities, has become an essential element in civil, scientific, and military space development because of the emergence of a United States commercial industry which provides Global Positioning System equipment and related services.

(b) INTERNATIONAL COOPERATION.—In order to support and sustain the Global Positioning System in a manner that will most effectively contribute to the national security, public safety, scientific, and economic interests of the United States, the Congress encourages the President to—

(1) ensure the operation of the Global Positioning System on a continuous worldwide basis free of direct user fees;

(2) enter into international agreements that promote cooperation with foreign governments and international organizations to—

(A) establish the Global Positioning System and its augmentations as an acceptable international standard; and

(B) eliminate any foreign barriers to applications of the Global Positioning System worldwide; and (3) provide clear direction and adequate resources to the Assistant Secretary of Commerce for Communications and Information so that on an international basis the Assistant Secretary can—

(A) achieve and sustain efficient management of the electromagnetic spectrum used by the Global Positioning System; and

(B) protect that spectrum from disruption and interference.

SEC. 105. ACQUISITION OF SPACE SCIENCE DATA.

(a)ACQUISITION FROM COMMERCIAL PROVIDERS.—The Administrator shall, to the extent possible and while satisfying the scientific or

152

educational requirements of the National Aeronautics and Space Administration, and where appropriate, of other Federal agencies and scientific researchers, acquire, where cost effective, space science data from a commercial provider.

(b) TREATMENT OF SPACE SCIENCE DATA AS COMMERCIAL ITEM UNDER ACQUISITION LAWS.—Acquisitions of space science data by the Administrator shall be carried out in accordance with applicable acquisition laws and regulations (including chapters 137 and 140 of title 10, United States Code). For purposes of such law and regulations, space science data shall be considered to be a commercial item. Nothing in this subsection shall be construed to preclude the United States from acquiring, through contracts with commercial providers, sufficient rights in data to meet the needs of the scientific and educational community or the needs of other government activities.

(c)DEFINITION.—For purposes of this section, the term "space science data" includes scientific data concerning—

(1) the elemental and mineralogical resources of the moon, asteroids, planets and their moons, and comets;

(2) microgravity acceleration; and

(3) solar storm monitoring.

(d) SAFETY STANDARDS.— Nothing in this section shall be construed to prohibit the Federal Government from requiring compliance with applicable safety standards.

(e)LIMITATION.—This section does not authorize the National Aeronautics and Space Administration to provide financial assistance for the development of commercial systems for the collection of space science data.

SEC. 106. ADMINISTRATION OF COMMERCIAL SPACE CENTERS.

The Administrator shall administer the Commercial Space Center program in a coordinated manner from National Aeronautics and Space Administration headquarters in Washington, D.C.

SEC. 107. SOURCES OF EARTH SCIENCE DATA.

(a)ACQUISITION.—The Administrator shall, to the extent possible and while satisfying the scientific or educational requirements of the National Aeronautics and Space Administration, and where appropriate, of other Federal agencies and scientific researchers, acquire, where cost-effective, space-based and airborne Earth remote sensing data, services, distribution, and applications from a commercial provider.

(b) TREATMENT AS COMMERCIAL ITEM UNDER ACQUISITION LAWS.—Acquisitions by the Administrator of the data, services, distribution, and applications referred to in subsection (a) shall be carried out in accordance with applicable acquisition laws and regulations (including chapters 137 and 140 of title 10, United States Code). For purposes of such law and regulations, such data, services, distribution, and applications shall be considered to be a commercial item. Nothing in this subsection shall be construed to preclude the United States from acquiring, through contracts with commercial providers, sufficient rights in data to meet the needs of the scientific and educational community or the needs of other government activities.

(c)STUDY.—(1) The Administrator shall conduct a study to determine the extent to which the baseline scientific requirements of Earth Science can be met by commercial providers, and how the National Aeronautics and Space Administration will meet such requirements which cannot be met by commercial providers.

(2) The study conducted under this subsection shall—

(A) make recommendations to promote the availability of information from the National Aeronautics and Space Administration to commercial providers to enable commercial providers to better meet the baseline scientific requirements of Earth Science;

(B) make recommendations to promote the dissemination to commercial providers of

154

information on advanced technology research and development performed by or for the National
Aeronautics and Space Administration; and

    (C) identify policy, regulatory, and legislative barriers to the implementation of the recommendations made under this subsection.

    (3) The results of the study conducted under this subsection shall be transmitted to the Congress within 6 months after the date of the enactment of this Act.

    (d) SAFETY STANDARDS.— Nothing in this section shall be construed to prohibit the Federal Government from requiring compliance with applicable safety standards.

    (e)ADMINISTRATION AND EXECUTION.—This section shall be carried out as part of the Commercial Remote Sensing Program at the Stennis Space Center.

    (f)REMOTE SENSING.—

    (1) APPLICATION CONTENTS.— Section 201(b) of the Land Remote Sensing Policy Act of 1992 (15 U.S.C. 5621(b)) is amended—

        (A) by inserting "(1)" after "NATIONAL SECURITY.—"; and

        (B) by adding at the end the following new paragraph:

"(2) The Secretary, within 6 months after the date of the enactment of the Commercial Space Act of 1998, shall publish in the Federal Register a complete and specific list of all information required to comprise a complete application for a license under this title. An application shall be considered complete when the applicant has provided all information required by the list most recently published in the Federal Register before the date the application was first submitted. Unless the Secretary has, within 30 days after receipt of an application, notified the applicant of information necessary to complete an application, the Secretary may not deny the application on the basis of the absence of any such information.".

(2) NOTIFICATION OF AGREEMENTS.—Section 202(b)(6) of the Land Remote Sensing Policy Act of 1992 (15 U.S.C. 5622(b)(6)) is amended by inserting "significant or substantial" after "Secretary of any".

TITLE II—FEDERAL ACQUISITION OF SPACE TRANSPORTATION SERVICES

SEC. 201. REQUIREMENT TO PROCURE COMMERCIAL SPACE TRANSPORTATION SERVICES.

(a)IN GENERAL.—Except as otherwise provided in this section, the Federal Government shall acquire space transportation services from United States commercial providers whenever such services are required in the course of its activities. To the maximum extent practicable, the Federal Government shall plan missions to accommodate the space transportation services capabilities of United States commercial providers.

(b) EXCEPTIONS.—The Federal Government shall not be required to acquire space transportation services under subsection (a) if, on a case-by-case basis, the Administrator or, in the case of a national security issue, the Secretary of the Air Force, determines that—

(1) a payload requires the unique capabilities of the Space Shuttle;

(2) cost effective space transportation services that meet specific mission requirements would not be reasonably available from United States commercial providers when required;

(3) the use of space transportation services from United States commercial providers poses an unacceptable risk of loss of a unique scientific opportunity;

(4) the use of space transportation services from United States commercial providers is inconsistent with national security objectives;

(5) the use of space transportation services from United States commercial providers is inconsistent with international agreements for international collaborative efforts relating to science and technology;

(6) it is more cost effective to transport a payload in conjunction with a test or demonstration of a space transportation vehicle owned by the Federal Government; or

(7) a payload can make use of the available cargo space on a Space Shuttle mission as a secondary payload, and such payload is consistent with the requirements of research, development, demonstration, scientific, commercial, and educational programs authorized by the Administrator. Nothing in this section shall prevent the Administrator from planning or negotiating agreements with foreign entities for the launch of Federal Government payloads for international collaborative efforts relating to science and technology.

(c)DELAYED EFFECT.—Subsection (a) shall not apply to space transportation services and space transportation vehicles acquired or owned by the Federal Government before the date of the enactment of this Act, or with respect to which a contract for such acquisition or ownership has been entered into before such date.

(d) HISTORICAL PURPOSES.—This section shall not be construed to prohibit the Federal Government from acquiring, owning, or maintaining space transportation vehicles solely for historical display purposes.

SEC. 202. ACQUISITION OF COMMERCIAL SPACE TRANSPORTATION SERVICES.

(a) TREATMENT OF COMMERCIAL SPACE TRANSPORTATION SERVICES AS COMMERCIAL ITEM UNDER ACQUISITION LAWS.—Acquisitions of space transportation services by the Federal Government shall be carried out in accordance with applicable acquisition laws and regulations (including chapters 137 and 140 of title 10, United States Code). For purposes of such law and regulations, space transportation services shall be considered to be a commercial item.

(b)   SAFETY STANDARDS.—

Nothing in this section shall be construed to prohibit the Federal Government from requiring compliance with applicable safety standards.

SEC. 203. LAUNCH SERVICES PURCHASE ACT OF 1990 AMENDMENTS. The Launch Services Purchase Act of 1990 (42 U.S.C. 2465b et seq.) is amended—

(1) by striking section 202;

(2) in section 203—

(A)   by striking paragraphs (1) and (2); and

(B)   by redesignating paragraphs (3) and (4) as paragraphs (1) and (2), respectively;

(3) by striking sections 204 and 205; and

(4) in section 206—

(A)   by striking "(a) COMMERCIAL PAYLOADS ON THE SPACE SHUTTLE.—"; and

(B)   by striking subsection (b).

SEC. 204. SHUTTLE PRIVATIZATION.

(a)POLICY AND PREPARATION.—The Administrator shall prepare for an orderly transition from the Federal operation, or Federal management of contracted operation, of space transportation systems to the Federal purchase of commercial space transportation services for all nonemergency space transportation requirements for transportation to and from Earth orbit, including human, cargo, and mixed payloads. In those preparations, the Administrator shall take into account the need for short-term economies, as well as the goal of restoring the National Aeronautics and Space Administration's research focus and its mandate to promote the fullest possible commercial use of space. As part of those preparations, the

Administrator shall plan for the potential privatization of the Space Shuttle program. Such plan shall keep safety and cost effectiveness as high priorities. Nothing in this section shall prohibit the National Aeronautics and Space Administration from studying, designing, developing, or funding upgrades or modifications essential to the safe and economical operation of the Space Shuttle fleet.

(b)   FEASIBILITY   STUDY.—The Administrator shall conduct a study of the feasibility of implementing the recommendation of the Independent Shuttle Management Review Team that the National Aeronautics and Space Administration transition toward the privatization of the Space Shuttle. The study shall identify, discuss, and, where possible, present options for resolving, the major policy and legal issues that must be addressed before the Space Shuttle is privatized, including—

(1)   whether the Federal Government or the Space Shuttle contractor should own the Space Shuttle orbiters and ground facilities;

(2)   whether the Federal Government should indemnify the contractor for any third party liability arising from Space Shuttle operations, and, if so, under what terms and conditions;

(3)   whether payloads other than National Aeronautics and Space Administration payloads should be allowed to be launched on the Space Shuttle, how missions will be prioritized, and who will decide which mission flies and when;

(4)   whether commercial payloads should be allowed to be launched on the Space Shuttle and whether any classes of payloads should be made ineligible for launch consideration;

(5)   whether National Aeronautics and Space Administration and other Federal Government payloads should have priority over non-Federal payloads in the Space Shuttle launch assignments, and what policies should

be developed to prioritize among payloads generally;

(6) whether the public interest requires that certain Space Shuttle functions continue to be performed by the Federal Government; and

(7) how much cost savings, if any, will be generated by privatization of the Space Shuttle.

(c)REPORT TO CONGRESS.—Within 60 days after the date of the enactment of this Act, the National Aeronautics and Space Administration shall complete the study required under subsection (b) and shall submit a report on the study to the Committee on Commerce, Science, and Transportation of the Senate and the Committee on Science of the House of Representatives.

SEC. 205. USE OF EXCESS INTERCONTINENTAL BALLISTIC MISSILES. (a) IN GENERAL.—The Federal Government shall not—

(1) convert any missile described in subsection (c) to a space transportation vehicle configuration; or

(2) transfer ownership of any such missile to another person, except as provided in subsection (b).

(b) AUTHORIZED FEDERAL USES.—(1) A missile described in subsection (c) may be converted for use as a space transportation vehicle by the Federal Government if, except as provided in paragraph (2) and at least 30 days before such conversion, the agency seeking to use the missile as a space transportation vehicle transmits to the Committee on National Security and the Committee on Science of the House of Representatives, and to the Committee on Armed Services and the Committee on Commerce, Science, and Transportation of the Senate, a certification that the use of such missile—

(A) would result in cost savings to the Federal Government when compared to the cost of acquiring space transportation services from United States commercial providers;

(B)   meets all mission requirements of the agency, including performance, schedule, and risk requirements;

(C)   is consistent with international obligations of the United States; and

(D)   is approved by the Secretary of Defense or his designee.

(2) The requirement under paragraph (1) that the certification described in that paragraph must be transmitted at least 30 days before conversion of the missile shall not apply if the Secretary of Defense determines that compliance with that requirement would be inconsistent with meeting immediate national security requirements.

(c) MISSILES REFERRED TO.— The missiles referred to in this section are missiles owned by the United States that—

(1)   were formerly used by the Department of Defense for national defense purposes as intercontinental ballistic missiles; and

(2)   have been declared excess to United States national defense needs and are in compliance with international obligations of the United States.

SEC. 206. NATIONAL LAUNCH CAPABILITY STUDY.

(a)   FINDINGS.—Congress finds that a robust satellite and launch industry in the United States serves the interest of the United States by—

(1)   contributing to the economy of the United States;

(2)   strengthening   employment, technological, and scientific interests of the United States; and

(3)   serving the foreign policy and national security interests of the United States.

(b)   DEFINITIONS.—In this section:

(1)   SECRETARY.—The   term "Secretary" means the Secretary of Defense.

(2)   TOTAL POTENTIAL NATIONAL MISSION MODEL.—The term "total potential

national mission model" means a model that—
(A) is determined by the Secretary, in consultation with the Administrator, to assess the total potential space missions to be conducted in the United States during a specified period of time; and
(B) includes all launches in the United States (including launches conducted on or off a Federal range).

(c)   REPORT.—

(1)   IN GENERAL.—Not later than 180 days after the date of enactment of this Act, the Secretary shall, in consultation with the Administrator and appropriate representatives of the satellite and launch industry and the governments of States and political subdivisions thereof—

    (A)   prepare a report that meets the requirements of this subsection; and

    (B)   submit that report to the Committee on Commerce, Science, and Transportation of the Senate and the Committee on Science of the House of Representatives.

(2)   REQUIREMENTS   FOR REPORT.—The report prepared under this subsection shall—

    (A)   identify the total potential national mission model for the period beginning on the date of the report and ending on December 31, 2007;

    (B)   identify the resources that are necessary or available to carry out the total potential national mission model described in subparagraph (A), including—

        (i)   launch property and services of the Department of Defense, the National Aeronautics and Space Administration, and non-Federal facilities; and

        (ii)   the ability to support commercial launch-on-demand on short notification, taking into account Federal requirements, at launch sites or test ranges in the United States;

(C)   identify each deficiency in the resources referred to in subparagraph (B); and

(D)   with respect to the deficiencies identified under subparagraph (C), include estimates of the level of funding necessary to address those deficiencies for the period described in subparagraph (A).

(d)   RECOMMENDATIONS.—Based on the reports under subsection (c), the Secretary, after consultation with the Secretary of Transportation, the Secretary of Commerce, and representatives from interested private sector entities, States, and local governments, shall—

(1)   identify opportunities for investment by non-Federal entities (including States and political subdivisions thereof and private sector entities) to assist the Federal Government in providing launch capabilities for the commercial space industry in the United States;

(2)   identify one or more methods by which, if sufficient resources referred to in subsection (c)(2)(D) are not available to the Department of Defense and the National Aeronautics and Space Administration, the control of the launch property and launch services of the Department of Defense and the National Aeronautics and Space Administration may be transferred from the Department of Defense and the National Aeronautics and Space Administration to— (A) one or more other Federal agencies;

(B)   one or more States (or subdivisions thereof);

(C)   one or more private sector entities; or

(D)   any combination of the entities described in subparagraphs (A) through (C); and

(3)   identify the technical, structural, and legal impediments associated with making launch sites or test ranges in the United States viable and competitive.

Speaker of the House of Representatives.
Vice President of the United States and President of the Senate.

Glossary of Space Related Terms

Aerospace Safety Advisory Panel or ***ASAP*** – A panel that is supposed to advise the NASA administrator about the dangers of various systems and evaluates proposed safety standards.

Aldrin Mars Cycler – An ingeniously elegant-but-simple system of vehicles in an orbit around the Sun that would continually traverse the distance between Earth and Mars; thereby, allowing economical transportation between the two planets with minimal expenditure of propellant. The concept was invented by former Apollo astronaut Edwin (Buzz) Aldrin.

Apollo – The U.S. program to land people on the Moon. Each Apollo spacecraft flew three astronauts to the Moon. One of the astronauts would stay in orbit around the Moon in the Apollo Command Module spacecraft while the other two would descend in a LEM to the Moon's surface, explore, and then return in the LEM to their partner waiting in lunar orbit. After that they would return back to Earth.

Apollo Command Module – The main spacecraft that U.S. astronauts used to travel from the Earth to the Moon. Attached to it was the Service Module that supplied life-support functions and extra rocket power needed for leaving Earth orbit entering lunar orbit and leaving lunar orbit when returning back to Earth.

Ares-1 – A launcher that was being built under project Constellation and was to be constructed from Space Shuttle hardware. It was meant to allow astronauts in the Orion space capsule to go to either the ISS or to rendezvous with vehicles used for travelling to the Moon. Ares-1 was cancelled before the first one was ever finished because of budget overruns and technical problems that would have required excessively costly solutions. It was sometimes referred to as *The Corndog* because of its striking resemblance to the popular American fast-food of the same name.

Ares-1X – A rocket which resembled an Ares-1 launch vehicle in appearance, though in reality its physical characteristics and functional features had little in common with the proposed Ares-1. It was launched to a low altitude once in 2009. This flight is the source of the misconception (held by some) that an actual Ares-1 flew at least once.

Ares-V – A SD HLLV originally proposed for the now defunct return-to-the-Moon project called Constellation. Due to the efforts of some pork seeking politicians, Ares-V has been reborn as the so-called *Space Launch System*.

ASAP – See *Aerospace Safety Advisory Panel*.

Associate Administrator for Exploration Systems – The NASA official whose primary responsibility is determining and recommending what human spaceflight and exploration methods should be employed to yield the most efficient, effective and practical use, given NASA's specific amount of funds budgeted for that purpose. This person is supposed to be the NASA administrator's primary advisor on such matters.

Asteroid – A relatively small rocky body orbiting around the Sun that is essentially debris left over from the formation of the planets. Typically, they range in size from a few meters to hundreds of kilometers wide. Most of these objects lie in the Asteroid Belt between the orbits of Mars and Jupiter. However, Jupiter's gravity has flung many of these objects in the direction of Earth (see NEO) and in the other direction into the outer Solar System.

Asteroid Belt – The area between the orbits of Mars and Jupiter where the majority of asteroids exist. However, some asteroids orbit the Sun outside of this zone, a certain number of which come close to Earth. (See NEA)

Atlas V – One of two EELVs originally developed to launch military and commercial satellites, this is the latest most advanced version of ULA's venerable Atlas line. Following the steps of its legendary ancestor *Atlas LV-3B* that launched John Glenn on the first American orbital flight in 1962, it is now slated to propel astronauts to ISS in CST-100 and Dream Chaser spacecraft. (See *Delta IV*)

Augustine Committee – See *Augustine Report*.

Augustine Report – A groundbreaking report that resulted from a study by a group of renowned space industry experts formally known as *The United States Human Space Flight Plans Committee* informally called the *Augustine Committee*. It was chaired by space industry icon *Norm Augustine*. The conclusions of this group gave credence to alternate methods of operation that NASA had not implemented before and ultimately provided much of the impetus for creating the Commercial Crew program.

Backside of the Moon – See *Far side of the Moon*

BDB – See *Big Dumb Booster*.

BEAM – See *Bigelow Expandable Activity Module*.

Beyond Low Earth Orbit – the volume of space far above LEO. Many consider geosynchronous orbit and beyond as BLEO.

Big Dumb Booster or ***BDB*** – A more simply built rocket booster that uses a less energy efficient design to put payloads in orbit more

166

cheaply. Don't let the use of the word "dumb" in the term fool you, it refers to *simplicity* not stupidity. This is actually a very intelligent and clever strategy. Because it is less efficient than a more optimized rocket, it is much bigger due to the need to hold much more propellant than a more efficient rocket and its payload is smaller for its size than for a more efficient rocket of the same size. Its engines and other hardware are *much cheaper* to produce than a more technically advanced rocket due to their lack of complexity because they are simpler to manufacture. A lower number of sophisticated parts means there is less to go wrong both in its manufacture and in operational flight, yielding a commensurate increase in reliability. Since the rocket hardware is of low cost and the extra needed rocket propellant is relatively cheap, the bigger rocket actually costs much less to use than a somewhat smaller more sophisticated rocket that could lift the same amount of payload. It is the intelligent use of *BDB*s by the Russians that have allowed them to undercut American launch prices for decades.

Bigelow Aerospace – A company specializing in manufacturing inflatable habitation and storage modules for orbital space stations. The modules can be used to build entire space stations or provide additional habitation and storage volume for ISS. Founded by hotel Magnate Robert Bigelow.

Bigelow Expandable Activity Module or **BEAM** – An inflatable expansion module for the ISS to be manufactured by Bigelow Aerospace that has a torus (or doughnut) shape. Because its deflated volume is very small compared to its final inflated volume, it can be launched on a standard commercial launch vehicle, inflated at ISS, and then attached to ISS. This module would greatly add to the usable volume of the ISS. Its unusual shape also allows unique applications beyond that of traditional space station modules.

BLEO – *Beyond Low Earth Orbit*

Booz-Allen-Hamilton Report – A report commissioned by NASA to evaluate the development and operational procedures for SLS. (Booz-Allen-Hamilton 2011)

CCiCap – See *Commercial Crew integrated Capability*.

CCP – See *Commercial Crew Program*.

Centrifugal Effect – The apparent pulling outward of an object that is moving around in a circular path which seems to give the object weight similar to a planet's gravitational field. It is sometimes erroneously referred to as centrifugal *force*, but it is **not** a force. Instead it is a *side-effect* of a *centripetal force* that prevents an object from travelling in a straight line as inertia constantly tries to make it do.

Centripetal force – The inward pulling force which holds a moving object in a circular path by attempting to pull it in toward the center of the circle and in so doing keeps it from flying away in a straight line due to its inertia. In the case of a satellite in orbit, gravity is the centripetal force. In the case of a spinning space station, the tensile strength of the outer wall of the station is the centripetal force which induces an effect called <u>centrifugal effect</u>, which appears to act in a similar manner to a planet's gravitational field.

Clark orbit – Another name for <u>geosynchronous orbit</u>. This term stems from the fact that British science popularizer and science fiction author Sir Arthur C. Clark first proposed using this orbit for communications satellites in 1948.

Comet - The following is somewhat of an oversimplification, but a comet is essentially a large chunk of dirty ice up to several miles in diameter that orbits around the Sun.

Commercial Crew integrated Capability or **CCiCap** - The first phase of the <u>Commercial Crew program</u> under which commercial rocket launchers and spacecraft are to be readied to safely carry humans into orbit.

Commercial Crew Program – Is a program sponsored by NASA to (in the agency's own official wording) "facilitate the development of a U.S. commercial crew space transportation capability, with the goal of achieving safe, reliable, and cost effective access to and from low-Earth orbit (LEO) and the ISS". In other words, NASA would help private companies develop new orbital launch vehicles and spacecraft; after which, NASA would purchase vehicles from these companies to transport astronauts to and from the ISS. These vehicles would be built to strict NASA safety specifications and would cost NASA much less money than if NASA had developed the vehicles and operated them itself. The manufacturers would also be able to use these vehicles for commercial passenger service to such destinations as a privately financed space station in orbit whose living space would consist of habitation modules produced by Bigelow Aerospace.

Constellation – NASA project that was supposed to return American astronauts to the Moon by the year 2020. Started in 2005 and cancelled in 2010 after it went tremendously over budget and studies indicated that it would only run up even greater bills while the targeted return to the Moon would have gotten pushed farther and farther into the future. Some politicians who were dissatisfied with the cancellation came up with SLS to keep their constituents who were working on Constellation employed, but independent studies and analyses have shown that SLS will probably be doomed to budget busting and cancellation as well.

Cost-Plus Contracting – NASA's traditional way of arranging payment to industry contractors during technology development projects. Under this type of contractual agreement, NASA must pay both for originally budgeted work and also for any work that was not specified in the budget. This often leads to massive cost overruns for the project under contract.

Crew Space Transportation-100 or **CST-100** – A capsule spacecraft proposed by Boeing for NASA's Commercial Crew Program that would transport astronauts to and from both the International Space Station and/or commercially produced Bigelow space stations. The CST-100 is slated to launch on ULA Atlas V launch vehicles.

CST-100 – See *Crew Space Transportation-100*

Delta IV – One of two EELVs originally developed to launch military and commercial satellites, this is the latest most advanced version of ULA's workhorse Delta line of launch vehicles. A very reliable and capable vehicle as one would expect from ULA. (see *Atlas V*)

Depot – See *propellant depot*.

Dragon – SpaceX's flagship spacecraft. Consists of two versions: one for hauling cargo to and from ISS, the other (called *Dragonrider*) designed to fly astronauts to ISS and other destinations and return them to Earth.

Dragonrider – The crewed version of SpaceX's *Dragon* spacecraft.

Dream Chaser – Sierra Nevada's flagship spacecraft. The only spaceplane spacecraft participating in NASA's Commercial Crew program for getting astronauts to and from the ISS and is also slated for passenger service for commercial Bigelow space stations. Like the Space Shuttle, it would land like an airplane on a runway. It is slated to be launched on ULA's Atlas V rocket. Dream Chaser is derived from NASA's *HL-10* experimental lifting body which in turn was inspired by the Soviet Union's *Bor-4* lifting body.

EELV – See *Evolved Expendable Launch Vehicle*.

ELV – See *Expendable Launch Vehicle*.

EML-2 – The L2 point in the Earth-Moon system. (see *Lagrangian point 2*)

Evolved Expendable Launch Vehicle or **EELV** – A later model ELV descended from an earlier model, but which is much more powerful and advanced than its predecessor as defined by the United States Air Force. Refers specifically to ULA's Atlas V and Delta IV launch vehicles.

Expendable Launch Vehicle or **ELV**– A rocket for putting spacecraft into orbit that is used once and thrown away. (see _RLV_)

F9 – See _Falcon 9_.

Falcon 9 or **F9** – A multi-purpose launch vehicle from SpaceX designed to launch cargo and astronauts to ISS as well as for putting both commercial and military satellites into orbit. Named after Han Solo's _Millenium Falcon_ of _Star Wars_ fame.

Falcon Heavy or **FH** – A huge powerful launch vehicle consisting of three _Falcon 9_ boosters and capable of launching twice the amount of payload to orbit as the Space Shuttle could. It is also powerful enough to allow advanced manned and robotic deep space missions.

FAR – See _Federal Acquisitions Regulations_.

Far side of the Moon – Also known as the _Backside of the Moon_. The half of the Moon that always faces away from Earth and as a result is never seen from Earth. This part of the Moon was not seen by human beings until 1959 when a Russian robotic spacecraft first photographed it. It is sometimes mistakenly called the _Darkside of the Moon_. Instead, the Moon's actual darkside is the part of the Moon that is _currently_ not lit by sunlight. As the Moon goes through its phases, every part of it gets its turn on the darkside. Thus, even the part of the Moon facing the Earth is at times the darkside of the moon.

Federal Acquisitions Regulations or **FAR** – A set of regulations that are useful in acquiring already developed spaceflight hardware, but can be overly restrictive if applied to the process of vehicle design and development. In the latter case, added red tape and micro-controlling oversight by NASA can make development costs much more expensive under a FAR based regime. One reason for higher expense is it gives NASA the ability to add features to a project at will; that is, features that were not originally agreed upon in the initial contract and which can cause huge added expenses leading to budget overruns. The combination of Cost-plus Contracting and FAR was one of several primary reasons that project Constellation became too expensive to continue and it also is a detrimental feature in the development of SLS for the same reasons. The negative aspects of FAR on vehicle development can be avoided through the use of _SAAs_.

FH – See _Falcon Heavy_.

Fuel – In rocket science this concept is somewhat different than in everyday life. It is best defined as one of the two energy supplying chemicals needed for a rocket to operate in the vacuum of space. The other energy supplying chemical is _oxidizer_.

Gateway – A proposed station located at <u>L2</u> that would act as a way-station for human exploration trips to the Moon or deeper into interplanetary space. One of its key features would be a depot for supplying spacecraft with the propellant they need to continue on to much farther destinations. It may also serve as a point where astronauts can transfer between spacecraft capable of taking off/landing on Earth and spacecraft more suitable for deep space travel.

Gemini – The second U.S. human spaceflight program in the mid-1960s which was to develop technologies and practice the operations in orbit that would be needed in the follow-up <u>Apollo</u> program. Instead of having one astronaut per spacecraft as in the Mercury project, Gemini spacecraft flew two astronauts.

Geostationary orbit – Another term for *Geosynchronous orbit*.

Geostationary Transfer Orbit – The trajectory a spacecraft takes from low Earth orbit to geosynchronous orbit. Not to be confused with *Geostationary Orbit*.

Geosynchronous orbit or **Geostationary Orbit** or <u>**Clark Orbit**</u> – Orbits located above the Earth's equator located at an altitude where a satellite will take 24 hours to complete an orbit. Since the Earth turns on its axis once every 24 hours, a satellite in geosynchronous orbit will appear to hang over one place on the Earth's surface. This property makes geosynchronous orbit a prime location for communications satellites because a dish antenna can be pointed at it once and will never need to be repointed. The altitude of the orbit is some 23,000 miles above the Earth's surface.

Grasshopper – A program being conducted by SpaceX in an attempt to gradually modify both stages of its Falcon 9 booster for reusability over multiple flights. Actual test flights are being done with Falcon 9 stages modified with landing gear and capable of taking off, returning from flight, and landing under rocket power.

Gravity well – The volume of space around a large astronomical body (such as a planet or a moon) where the body's gravitational pull is strong enough to significantly alter the path of a spacecraft.

GTO – See *Geostationary Transfer Orbit*.

Heavy Lift Launch Vehicle or **HLLV** – Same as *Heavy Lift Vehicle*.

Heavy Lift Vehicle or **HLV** – The largest most massive category of launch vehicle. To qualify as an HLV, a rocket must be capable of putting *at least* 50,000 kg of payload into LEO according to the *Augustine Report*.

HLLV – See *Heavy Lift Launch Vehicle*

HLV – See *Heavy Lift Vehicle*.

ISS – The *International Space Station*.

L2 – See *Lagrangian point 2*.

Lagrangian point 2 – Also known as *L2*. One of five *Lagrangian points* in outer space numbered L1 through L5. In the case of the Earth-Moon system, L2 is the place beyond the backside of the Moon where the gravitational pull of the Earth and the Moon cancel each other. Thus, any object residing there has a general tendency to stay put in a relatively stable location requiring only minimal and infrequent expenditure of propellant to maintain its position in space. This relative stability makes L2 a great place for a deep space supply dock or a deep space propellant depot. It should be more properly referred to as *Earth-Moon L2* or *EML-2*, since there is also a *Sun-Earth L2* or SE-2 where the gravitational pull of the Sun and the Earth balance each other in a similar manner. In the case of SE-2, the L2 point is farther away from the Sun than the Earth above our planet's night side.

Lagrangian points – Places where the gravitational pull of two celestial bodies cancel each other. In the case of the Earth-Moon system, *Lagrange 1 (L1)* is the point between Earth and the Moon where this condition occurs, *L2* is the gravitational balance point beyond the Moon, *L3* is the balance point beyond the opposite side of Earth from the Moon, *L4* is the balance point 60 degrees ahead in the Moon in its orbit, whilst L5 is the one 60 degrees behind the Moon's orbital position. These places are named after the brilliant French scientist *Joseph Louis Lagrange* who first imagined their existence and calculated their characteristics in the year 1772.

LAS – See *Launch Abort System*.

Launch Abort System or **LAS** – See *Launch Escape System*.

Launch Escape System – The rocket powered system that allows a spacecraft containing human occupants to accelerate away from the booster that is transporting it to orbit in the event of an emergency and safely return the crew to Earth.

LEM – See *Lunar Excursion Module*.

LEO – See *Low Earth Orbit*.

LES – See *Launch Escape System*.

Lifting body – A relatively narrow oblong shaped vehicle with a round blunted nose whose entire body acts as a wing when it is flying through the air. Proposed as a spacecraft that would have more freedom of movement in the Earth's atmosphere than a traditional space capsule; thereby, offering a returning crew a greater number of landing site choices. The idea behind the lifting body was originally proposed in 1957 by Dr. Alfred J. Eggers Jr. at Ames Aeronautical laboratory (now NASA Ames Research Center).

Liquid oxygen – Also called *LOX*. Pure oxygen made so cold that it becomes a concentrated liquid. Used to supply the oxygen needed to burn rocket fuel in space where there is no air.

LOC – See *Loss of Crew estimate*.

Loss of Crew estimate or **LOC** – A calculated educated guess of the probability that a fatal accident will occur on any particular flight.

Low Earth Orbit - The volume of space very near the Earth where low altitude satellites (such as ISS) orbit.

LOX – See *Liquid Oxygen*.

Lunar Excursion Module – The lander spacecraft that allowed Apollo astronauts to land on the Moon and return to the *Apollo Command Module* waiting in lunar orbit.

Mercury – The first U.S. human spaceflight project whose operations began with Alan Shepherd's short suborbital flight in 1961 and progressed to the first American orbital flight of John Glenn and further manned orbital flights in the project through 1963.

MMSEV – See *Multi-Mission Space Exploration Vehicle*.

More Politically Correct Vehicle – Derogatory name for the spacecraft known at NASA as the *Multi-Purpose Crew Vehicle*. A result of the claim by some that it costs billions more than it should to maximize pork barrel spending.

MPCV – See *Multi-Purpose Crew Vehicle*.

Multi-Mission Space Exploration Vehicle or **MMSEV** – An alternate designation for *NAUTILUS-X*.

Multi-Purpose Crew Vehicle or **MPCV** – Spacecraft developed by NASA for the stated purpose of deep space travel. The pressurized capsule part of this spacecraft is officially designated as *Orion*.

National Space Council or **NSC** – A cabinet level council during the administration of G.H.W. Bush which was the successor to the National Aeronautics and Space Council that existed under previous administrations. Its purpose was to formulate and implement presidential policy related to spaceflight.

NAUTILUS-X – See *Non-Atmospheric Universal Transport Intended for Lengthy United States eXploration*.

NEA – See *Near Earth Asteroid*.

Near Earth Asteroid or **NEA** – The type of *Near Earth Object* that is an asteroid rather than a comet.

Near Earth Object or **NEO** – An asteroid or comet whose orbit frequently brings it close to the vicinity of Earth. Because of their proximity, some of them are considered prime candidates as a destination for the first human deep space missions beyond the Moon.

NEO – See <u>Near Earth Object</u>.

Non-Atmospheric Universal Transport Intended for Lengthy United States eXploration or **NAUTILUS-X** – A NASA proposal to produce the world's first *true* spaceship for frontier exploration into the depths of space. The ship would stay in space and never land. It would also have "artificial gravity" via <u>centrifugal effect</u> for the comfort and health of crew and passengers as well as extensive radiation protection. It is also often referred to by the alternate designation of *MMSEV*. Unfortunately, it is not likely to happen as long as SLS is being financed.

NSC – See <u>National Space Council</u>.

OCT – See <u>Office of the Chief Technologist</u>.

Office of the Chief Technologist or **OCT** – The part of NASA that is "responsible for direct management of NASA's Space Technology programs and for coordination and tracking of all technology investments across the agency."
http://www.nasa.gov/offices/oct/about_us/index.html

Orbital Sciences – A major manufacturer of satellite launch vehicles in the United States. They are one of two U.S. companies that supply ISS with their *Antares* launch vehicle and *Cygnus* spacecraft.

Orion – Name of the NASA capsule spacecraft being developed to take astronauts to the vicinity of the Moon and beyond. This capsule is the crew living quarters part of the <u>MPCV</u> and is also the vehicle that would return astronauts back to Earth.

Oxidizer – The chemical that supplies the oxygen needed for rocket fuel to burn. In space where there is no air and hence no oxygen, a conventional rocket must carry its own supply of oxygen in the form of oxidizer. The most common oxidizer is <u>LOX</u>, but can also be red fuming nitric acid, hydrogen peroxide, and any other chemical that can supply oxygen to the fuel to allow it to burn rapidly.

Phenolic Impregnated Carbon Ablator or **PICA** – A heat shield material developed at NASA's Ames Research Center that is light weight and able to withstand much greater stress and heat during atmospheric reentry than previously used materials. (<u>Tran et al. 1997</u>)

PICA – See <u>Phenolic Impregnated Carbon Ablator</u>

Propellant – Chemicals which when combined and ignited cause a rocket or spacecraft to be propelled forward. Propellant consists of two parts: *fuel* and *oxidizer*.

Propellant Depot – A permanent in-space installation for filling spacecraft with propellant so that they can continue on to destinations deeper in space. The spaceflight equivalent of a gas station in relation to cars and trucks. Such filling stations would be located in convenient places (such as a *gateway*) that maximize their usefulness at both LEO and L2.

RBS – See *Reusable Booster System*

Reusable Booster System or **RBS** – A now defunct Air Force project that contracted several major aerospace companies to develop a quick response two stage reusable satellite launcher.

Reusable Launch Vehicle or **RLV** – A rocket that launches spacecraft into orbit that can be reused multiple times. Costs more up front to build, but is supposed to be cheaper to operate than an ELV or EELV. Regardless of what some think, the Shuttle was not a true RLV because it was not totally reusable.

Reusable Solid Rocket Motor – A solid rocket motor proposed by ATK in response to the proposed booster competition for SLS Block 2.

RLV – See *Reusable Launch Vehicle*.

Rocket Equation, The – A formula used to determine what percentage of a rocket's initial weight at lift-off can be payload. Because of limitations governed by the physics of a rocket launch, the payload mass fraction will be no more than 2% to 3% of the entire rocket's mass at launch. However, due to design compromises implemented for economic reasons, the fraction that can be usable payload is typically closer to a range of 1% to 1½%.

Rocket to Nowhere or **RTN** – Pejorative nickname for the SLS. So called because it is so expensive that it takes away the money needed to develop the huge payloads it was designed to launch.

RSRM – see *Reusable Solid Rocket Motor*.

RTN – See *Rocket to Nowhere*.

SAA – See *Space Act Agreement*

Saturn 1B – The first large booster developed for project Apollo built to do orbital testing of Apollo spacecraft systems before the Saturn V was completed. There were two unmanned launches of this vehicle before it actually launched astronauts into Earth orbit on the Apollo 7 mission.

Saturn V – The giant rocket built by NASA during the Apollo project that sent astronauts to the Moon in the 1960s. There has never been a rocket before or since that was as powerful. SLS theoretically would be more powerful, but the Booz-Allen-Hamilton report states that it will continually fall behind schedule in around 3 to 5 years and possibly never reach operational status.

SD HLLV – See *Shuttle-derived Heavy Lift Launch Vehicle*.

SD HLV – See *Shuttle-derived Heavy Lift Launch Vehicle*.

Senate Launch System – Derogatory nickname for SLS. This moniker stems from the fact that a few members of the Senate drew up a bill which dictates what technologies may be used to build SLS in an attempt to make sure the primary beneficiaries of the project were their constituents.

Shuttle-derived Heavy Lift Launch Vehicle or **SD HLLV** or **SD HLV** – A large HLV built using technology that was used in the Space Shuttle such as *SLS* or the now cancelled *Ares V*.

SLS – See *Space Launch System*.

Space Act Agreement or **SAA** – A contractual agreement between NASA and a company that allows development of spaceflight hardware to prevent the use of procedures required under a <u>FAR</u> agreement in situations where FAR is non-essential and would actually *slow* development progress and be *more costly* **without** giving a commensurate advantage from the standpoint of safety and other important metrics.

Space Anti-Leadership Act, The – See *Space Leadership Act, The*

Space Exploration Technologies – Also known as *SpaceX*. The company that produces the *Falcon 9* and *Falcon Heavy* launchers as well as the *Dragon* spacecraft. For a long time, some people either thought or (for political expediency) proclaimed SpaceX was the only rocket company that would be supplying launchers for NASA's Commercial Crew program that will cease our reliance on Russia to launch our astronauts into space. In reality, *ULA* was always going to be part of the mix by also supplying launchers for this program.

Space Launch System or **SLS** - A giant rocket that is being built with technology mostly derived from Space Shuttle and Apollo era technology and claimed (by its supporters) to be a practical way of sending people to the Moon and beyond.

Space Leadership Act, The – A proposed piece of legislation that would give Congress greater power to prevent a sitting President from either removing a NASA Administrator from office or cancelling a useless project, thus lessening the probability a pet space program will be cancelled which is wasting taxpayer money (such as the now defunct Project Constellation and the currently existing SLS development project). Given that fact, it is often referred to by it its opponents as the *Space Anti-Leadership Act*.

SpaceX – See *Space Exploration Technologies*.

TAAT – See *Technology Application Assessment Team*.

Technology Application Assessment Team or **TAAT** – A group of scientists and engineers at NASA whose job it is to determine the feasibility of implementing a new technology.

TLI – See *Trans-Lunar Insertion*.

Trans-Lunar Insertion or **TLI** – The rocket firing necessary to start a spacecraft on its journey from low Earth orbit to the Moon's vicinity.

ULA – See *United Launch Alliance*.

United Launch Alliance or **ULA** – Manufacturers of the *Atlas* and *Delta* launch vehicles that have been continuously improved and modernized since their inception in the 1960's. These are the trusty workhorse launchers that America has always relied on to orbit the state of the art GPS, communications, and reconnaissance satellites that are part of the backbone of U.S. military might. ULA is now supplying launch vehicles for NASA's Commercial Crew program.

United Space Alliance or **USA** – The company (equally owned by Boeing and Lockheed) that formerly refurbished, launched and maintained the now retired Space Shuttle for NASA. Not to be confused with ULA.

USA – See *United Space Alliance*

Vaporware – A term aerospace engineering has borrowed from computer science. Specifically, it refers to a touted project that is given much publicity, but has little or no chance of resulting in a finished fully functional product.

Venture Star or **X-33** – An unmanned suborbital combined launcher/spacecraft that was to be the test prototype of NASA's next generation reusable orbital launch system to replace the Space Shuttle. Started in 1996 and cancelled in 2001 after technical and funding difficulties were encountered.

X-33 - See *Venture Star*.

X-34 – An unmanned suborbital space plane that was to be a test bed for new technologies to be used on orbital crewed vehicles. The project was cancelled in 2001.

References

Aldrin a, Buzz; 2012; "American Space Exploration Leadership – Why and How", *The Huffington Post*, Washington, DC, January 5 http://www.huffingtonpost.com/buzz-aldrin/american-space-exploration b 1184554.html last online access March 13, 2013

Aldrin b, Buzz; 2009; "Why We Need Better Rockets", *The Huffington Post*, Washington, DC, November 9 http://www.huffingtonpost.com/buzz-aldrin/why-we-need-better-rocket b 351335.html last online access March 13, 2013

Amos, Jonathan; 2012; "SpaceX CEO Elon Musk: Europe's rocket 'has no chance'", *BBC News*, November 19 http://www.bbc.co.uk/news/science-environment-20389148 last online access March 13, 2013

Anderson 1a, Charlene; 2011; "The Skirmishing Has Just Begun", *The Planetary Society Website*, Pasadena, CA, July 12 http://planetary.org/blogs/emily-lakdawalla/2011/3096.html last online access March 13, 2013

Anderson 2a, Chris; 2012; "Elon Musk's Mission to Mars", *Wired.com*, October 21 http://www.wired.com/wiredscience/2012/10/ff-elon-musk-qa/all/ last online access March 13, 2013

Barr, Jonathan and Bernard Kutter; 2010; "Phase 2 EELV: An Old Configuration Option with New Relevance for Super Heavy Lift Cargo", *United Launch Alliance*, Centennial, Colorado http://www.ulalaunch.com/site/docs/publications/EELVPhase2 2010.pdf last online access March 13, 2013

Berger, Eric; 2012; "Expensive NASA rocket draws skepticism", *The Houston Chronicle*, Houston, Texas, January 28 http://www.chron.com/news/houston-texas/article/Laying-groundwork-or-a-gravestone-for-spaceflight-2795090.php last online access March 17, 2013

Bergin a, Chris; 2011; "Preliminary NASA plan shows evolved SLS vehicle at least 21 years away", *NASA Space Flight*, July 27 http://www.nasaspaceflight.com/2011/07/preliminary-nasa-evolved-sls-vehicle-21-years-away/ last online access March 13, 2013

Bergin b, Chris; 2012; "NASA safety panel call for crew risk mitigation via debut SLS mission", *NASASpaceflight.com*,

July 6 http://www.nasaspaceflight.com/2012/07/nasa-safety-panel-crew-risk-mitigation-debut-sls-mission/ last online access March 13, 2013

Bergin c, Chris; 2012; "Dynetics and PWR aiming to liquidize SLS booster competition with F-1 power", *NASASpaceflight.com*, November 9 http://www.nasaspaceflight.com/2012/11/dynetics-pwr-liquidize-sls-booster-competition-f-1-power/ last online access March 13, 2013

Bigelow Aerospace; 2012; "Genesis II", *BigelowAerospace.com*, las Vegas, Nevada, http://bigelowaerospace.com/genesis-2.php last online access March 13, 2013

Block, Robert; 2009; "Little Problems: NASA downplays Ares I-X damage",*The Orlando Sentinel,* Orlando, Florida, October 31, http://articles.orlandosentinel.com/2009-10-31/news/0910300168_1_ares-i-x-bob-ess-ares-i-rocket last online access March 13, 2013

Booz-Allen-Hamilton; 2011; *Independent Cost Assessment of the Space Launch System, Multi-purpose Crew Vehicle and 21st Century Ground Systems Programs: Executive Summary of Final Report,* NASA, Washington DC August 19 http://www.nasa.gov/pdf/581582main_BAH_Executive_Summary.pdf, page iv, last online access March 13, 2013

Boyle, Alan; 2012; "Beyond-the-Moon base stirs up buzz". *Cosmic Log,* NBC News, September 24 http://cosmiclog.nbcnews.com/_news/2012/09/24/14072181-beyond-the-moon-base-stirs-up-buzz last online access March 13, 2013

Braconnier, Deborah; 2011; "SpaceX plans to get humans to Mars", Phys.org, August 3 http://phys.org/news/2011-08-spacex-humans-mars.html last online access March 13, 2013

Clark a, Stephen; 2011; "Reduced Budget Threatens Delay in Private Spaceships", *Spaceflight Now Inc.*, November 23 http://spaceflightnow.com/news/n1111/23commercialcrew/ last online access March 13, 2013

Clark b, Stephen; 2010; "Second Falcon 9 rocket begins arriving at Cape", *Spaceflight Now Inc,* July 16 http://www.spaceflightnow.com/falcon9/002/100716firststage/ last online access March 13, 2013

Cowing a, Keith; 2011; "Sen. Hutchison & Staff Need To Learn to Read", *NASA Watch,* August 24 http://nasawatch.com/archives/2011/08/sen-hutchison-s.html last online access March 13, 2013

Cowing b, Keith; 2011; "Internal NASA Studies Show Cheaper and Faster Alternatives to The Space Launch System", *SpaceRef.com* October 12 http://www.spaceref.com/news/viewnews.html?id=1577 last online access March 13, 2013

Cowing c, Keith; 2011; "SpaceX Explains Why They Beat China on Cost", *NASA Watch,* May 4 http://nasawatch.com/archives/2011/05/spacex-explains.html last online access March 13, 2013

Cowing d, Keith; 2012; "Does SpaceX Makes Arianespace Nervous?", *NASA Watch*, November 12 http://nasawatch.com/archives/2012/11/does-spacex-mak.html last online access March 13, 2013

David, Leonard; 2010; "Bigelow Aerospace Soars with Private Space Station Deals", *Space.com*, October 19 http://www.space.com/9358-bigelow-aerospace-soars-private-space-station-deals.html last online access March 13, 2013

Dodson, Brian; 2012; "SpaceX's Grasshopper VTVL takes a 40 meter hop", *gizmag*, December 26 http://www.gizmag.com/spacex-grasshopper-vtvl-test/25562/ last online access March 13, 2013

Dyer a, Joseph W., James P. Bagian, Claude M. Bolton Jr., Robert E. Conway, John C. Frost, Donald P. McErlean, George C. Nield, Bryan D. O'Connor, Patricia A. Sanders; 2013; "Aerospace Safety Advisory Panel: Annual Report for 2012", NASA, Washington DC http://oiir.hq.nasa.gov/asap/documents/2013 ASAP Annual Report.pdf last online access March 13, 2013

Dyer b, Joseph W; 2012; "Statement of VADM Joseph W. Dyer, USN (Retired), Chairman National Aeronautics and Space Administration's Aerospace Safety Advisory Panel before the Committee on Science, Space, and Technology Subcommittee on Space and Aeronautics - U.S. House of Representatives", *NASA Office of International and Interagency Relations*, Washington DC, http://oiir.hq.nasa.gov/asap/documents/9-14-12 Dyer CCiCap Testimony.pdf last online access March 13, 2013

Eddington, Mark; 2010; "NASA Reauthorization Takes Solid Rocket Industry Off Life Support", *The Main Street Business Journal*, St George, Utah, Volume 13, Issue 29

Edwards, Ashley, Grey Hautaluoma, Kylie Clem; 2009; "NASA Selects Heat Shield for Orion Spacecraft Heatshield", *Press Release Archives*, NASA Headquarters, Washington DC, April 7 http://www.nasa.gov/home/hqnews/2009/apr/HQ 09-080 Orion Heat Shield.html last online access March 13, 2013

Ferster, Warren and Dan Leone; 2012; "SpaceX's Successful Mission Boosts Commercial Credibility", *Space News International*, Springfield, VA, May 25, http://www.spacenews.com/civil/120525-spacex-boosts-commercial-credibility.html last online access March 13, 2013 (behind paid firewall, subscription required)

Fleischauer, Eric; 2011; "Where are Tea Party's core beliefs?", *Decatur Daily*, Decatur, Alabama, April 17 http://www.decaturdaily.com/stories/Where-are-teapartys-core-beliefs,78238 last online access March 13, 2013

Fountain, Henry; 2013; "A Clearer View of the Space Bullet that Grazed Russia", *The New York Times*, March 25 http://www.nytimes.com/2013/03/26/science/space/in-asteroids-aftermath-a-sigh-of-relief.html?pagewanted=all&_r=0 Last online access March 25, 2013

Foust a, Jeff; 2012; "NASA's problem with Farmers, the Committee and Tinker Bells", *SpacePolitics.com*, June 30 http://www.spacepolitics.com/2012/06/30/nasas-problem-with-farmers-the-committee-and-tinkerbells/ last online access March 13, 2013

Foust b, Jeff; 2012; "Posey: "Going to the moon should be a goal" ", *SpacePolitics.com*, July 22 http://www.spacepolitics.com/2012/07/22/posey-going-to-the-moon-should-be-a-goal/ last online access March 13, 2013

Foust c, Jeff; 2012; "What is the future of the RLV?", *The Space Review*, November 26 http://www.thespacereview.com/article/2194/1 last online access March 13, 2013

Foust d, Jeff; 2009; "Conflicting guidance on ISS resupply funding", *SpacePolitics.com*, May 22 http://www.spacepolitics.com/2009/05/22/conflicting-guidance-on-iss-commercial-resupply-funding/ last online access March 13, 2013

Foust e, Jeff; 2013; "As sequestration goes into effect, revisiting its effects on NASA", *SpacePolitics.com*, Mar 2, http://www.spacepolitics.com/2013/03/02/as-sequestration-goes-into-effect-revisiting-its-effects-on-nasa last online access March 13, 2013

Foust f, Jeff; 2012; "Amendments to defense authorization bill cover export control and NASA policy", *SpacePolitics.com*, November 30, http://www.spacepolitics.com/2012/11/30/amendments-to-defense-authorization-bill-cover-export-control-and-nasa-policy/ last online access March 13, 2013

Foust g, Jeff; 2004; "NASA, the Air Force, and space transportation: room for cooperation?", *The Space Review*, April 5, http://www.thespacereview.com/article/126/1 last online access March 13, 2013

GAO; 2009; "Constellation Program Cost and Schedule Will Remain Uncertain Until a Sound Business Case Is Established", United States Government Accountability Office, Washington, DC http://www.gao.gov/new.items/d09844.pdf last online access March 13, 2013

Hennigan, W.J.; 2012; "A New Frontier for Space Travel", *Los Angeles Times*, Los Angeles, May 15 http://articles.latimes.com/2012/may/15/business/la-fi-spacex-launch-20120515 last online access March 13, 2013

Holderman, Mark; 2011; *NAUTILUS X: Multi-mission Deep Space Vehicle*, NASA Johnson Space Flight Center, Houston, Texas http://spirit.as.utexas.edu/~fiso/telecon/Holderman-Henderson_1-26-11/Holderman_1-26-11.ppt last online access March 13, 2013

HSF Architecture Team; 2011; *Propellant Depot Requirements Status Report*; NASA/Johnson Spaceflight Center, Houston, Texas, July 21 http://images.spaceref.com/news/2011/21.jul2011.vxs.pdf last online access March 13, 2013

Hutchison, Kay Bailey; 2012; "SA3078"; *Congressional Record*, The Library of Congress, Washington DC, November 28 http://www.gpo.gov/fdsys/pkg/CREC-2012-11-28/pdf/CREC-2012-11-28-pt1-PgS7045.pdf#page=27 last online access March 13, 2013

Keck Institute for Space Studies; 2012; "Asteroid Retrieval Feasibility Study", *California Institute of Technology*, April 2 http://www.kiss.caltech.edu/study/asteroid/asteroid_final_report.pdf last online access April 6, 2013

King, Leo; 2010; "Space Bill Moves on to Obama", *Examiner.com*, Denver, CO, September 30, http://www.examiner.com/article/space-bill-moves-on-to-obama-1 last online access March 13, 2013

Klingler a, Dave; 2012; "NASA Admin returns to Congress to fight for commercial space", *Ars Technica*, March 13 http://arstechnica.com/science/2012/03/nasa-admin-returns-to-congress-to-fight-for-commercial-space/ last online access March 13, 2013

Klingler b, Dave; 2012; "NASA's Commercial Crew gains support in Congress", *ars tehnica*, June 6 http://arstechnica.com/science/2012/06/nasas-commercial-crew-gains-support-in-congress/ last online access March 13, 2013

Kraft, Chris and Tom Moser; 2012; "Space Launch System is a threat to JSC, Texas jobs", *The Houston Chronicle*, Houston, April 20, http://www.chron.com/opinion/outlook/article/Space-Launch-System-is-a-threat-to-JSC-Texas-jobs-3498836.php last online access March 13, 2013

Leone, Dan; 2012; "NASA Plans to Add $375M to Lockheed's Orion Contract for Delta 4 Test", *SpaceNews.com*, January 9, http://www.spacenews.com/contracts/120109-nasa-add-375m-lockheed-orion-contract.html last online access March 13, 2013 (behind paid firewall, subscription required)

Lindsey a, Clark; 2012; "NASA safety panel reviews SLS/Orion", *New Space Watch*, July 6 http://www.newspacewatch.com/articles/nasa-safety-panel-reviews-slsorion.html last online access March 28, 2013

Lindsey b, Clark; 2013; "Bigelow Aerospace and NASA sign contract" *New Space Watch*, January 7 http://www.newspacewatch.com/articles/bigelow-aerospace-and-nasa-sign-contract.html last online access March 13, 2013

Lindsey c, Clark; 2013; "FISO: Skylab II – Making a deep space habitat from an SLS propellant tank", *Space For All*, March 28 http://hobbyspace.com/Blog/?p=1406 last online access March 28, 2013

Little, Geoffrey; 2008; "Mr. B's Big Plan"; *Air & Space Magazine*, January http://www.airspacemag.com/space-exploration/bigelow.html?c=y&page=4 last online access March 22, 2013

Luscombe, Richard; 2011; "NASA shows off 'most powerful space rocket in history'", *The Guardian*, London, September 14 http://www.guardian.co.uk/science/2011/sep/14/nasa-space-launch-system last online access March 13, 2013

Marks, Paul; 2013; "NASA buys blow-up habitat for space station astronauts"; *New Scientist*, January 16 http://www.newscientist.com/article/dn23083-nasa-buys-blowup-habitat-for-space-station-astronauts.html last online access March 13, 2013

Matthews a, Mark K.; 2011; "NASA's $10B rocket plan recycles shuttle parts, draws flak",*The Orlando Sentinel*, Orlando, Florida, May 15 http://articles.orlandosentinel.com/2011-05-15/news/os-nasa-recycled-shuttle-20110515_1_heavy-lift-rocket-rocket-plan-shuttle-parts last online access March 13, 2013

Matthews b, Mark K; 2012; "Sentinel Exclusive: NASA wants to send astronauts beyond the moon", *The Orlando Sentinel*, Orlando, Florida, September 22 http://articles.orlandosentinel.com/2012-09-22/news/os-nasa-space-outpost-20120922_1_moon-rocks-space-launch-system-nasa-chief-charlie-bolden last online access March 13, 2013

Matthews c, Mark K; 2010; "Shelby named 'porker' for protecting Constellation", *The Orlando Sentinel*, Orlando, Florida, June 22 http://blogs.orlandosentinel.com/news_space_thewritestuff/2010/06/shelby-named-%E2%80%98porker%E2%80%99-for-protecting-constellation.html last online access March 13, 2013

Messier a, Doug; 2011; "Shelby Supports SLS Competition While Contractors Worry in California", *Parabolic Arc*, June 16 http://www.parabolicarc.com/2011/06/16/shelby-supports-sls-competition-while-contractors-worry-california/ last online access March 13, 2013

Messier b, Doug; 2012; "Congress' Misleading Spaceflight Development Chart", *Parabolic Arc*, September 20 http://www.parabolicarc.com/2012/09/20/congress-misleading-human-spaceflight-development-chart/ last online access March 13, 2013

Miller, Charles; 2012; "How the US can become a next generation space industrial power", *The Space Review*, November 5 http://www.thespacereview.com/article/2184/1 last online access March 13, 2013

Money a, Stewart; 2012; "Why SpaceX is setting the pace in space", Special article to *NBC News*, July 30 http://www.msnbc.msn.com/id/48390277/ns/technology _and science-space/t/why-spacex-setting-pace-commercial-space-race/#.UGSky1HoCyI last online access March 13, 2013

Money b, Stewart; 2012; "NASA pushes for an L-2 outpost", *Innerspace.net*, September 26 http://innerspace.net/2012/09/26/nasa-pushes-for-an-l-2-outpost/ last online access March 13, 2013

Musk, Elon; 2011; "Why the US Can Beat China: The Facts About SpaceX Costs", *SpaceRef.com*, May 4 http://www.spaceref.com/news/viewpr.html?pid=33457 last online access March 13, 2013

NADAP (NASA Associate Deputy Administrator for Policy); 2011; "Falcon 9 Launch Vehicle NAFCOM Cost Estimates", *NASA*, Washington DC, August http://www.nasa.gov/pdf/586023main_8-3-11_NAFCOM.pdf last online access March 13, 2013

NASA a (National Aeronautics and Space Administration); 2012; "Space Launch System: Building America's Next Heavy Lift Launch Vehicle", *NASA Facts*, Marshall Space Flight Center, Huntsville, Alabama http://www.nasa.gov/pdf/664158main_sls_fs_master.pdf last online access March 13, 2013

NASA b (National Aeronautics and Space Administration); 2011; "Commercial Crew Program Forum", *NASA.gov*, John F. Kennedy Space Center, Florida http://commercialcrew.nasa.gov/document_file_get.cfm?docid=155 last online access March 13, 2013

NASA c (National Aeronautics and Space Administration); 2011; "Preliminary Report Regarding NASA's Space Launch System and Multi-Purpose Crew Vehicle", *NASA.gov*, Washington, DC, January http://www.nasa.gov/pdf/510449main_SLS_MPCV_90-day_Report.pdf last online access March 13, 2013.

National Academy of Sciences; 2013; "Committee on Human Spaceflight", *Aeronautics and Engineering Board*, Washington, D.C. http://sites.nationalacademies.org/DEPS/ASEB/DEPS_069080 last online access March 22, 2013

Nelson, Bill; 2013; "NASA has plan to capture an asteroid and tow it to the moon", April 5 http://www.billnelson.senate.gov/news/details.cfm?id=341278& last online access April 6, 2013

Newton, Kimberly; 2012; "NASA's Marshall Spaceflight Center Completes Wind Tunnel Testing for Sierra Nevada Corporation's Dream Chaser Spacecraft", *NASA.gov*, Marshall Spaceflight Center, Huntsville, Alabama, May 14 http://www.nasa.gov/centers/marshall/news/news/releases/2012/12-054.html last online access March 13, 2013

Newton, Kimberly; 2012; "NASA's Marshall Spaceflight Center Concludes Wind Tunnel Testing to Aid in SpaceX Reusable Launch System Design", *NASA.gov*, Marshall Spaceflight Center, Huntsville, Alabama, May 23 http://www.nasa.gov/centers/marshall/news/news/releases/2012/12-058.html last online access March 13, 2013

Posey a, Bill; 2012; "Reps. Posey, Culberson, Wolf and Olson introduce the Space Leadership Act", September 20 http://posey.house.gov/news/documentsingle.aspx?DocumentID=309399 last online access March 13, 2013

Posey b, Bill; 2011; "Posey Testimony to Budget Committee: Preserve Human Space Flight and Give NASA Clear Direction", March 30 http://posey.house.gov/news/documentsingle.aspx?DocumentID=232177 last online access March 13, 2013

Roop, Lee; 2010; "SpaceX's Elon Musk, Sen. Richard Shelby spar over Obama space policy", *The Huntsville Times*, Huntsville, Alabama, April 25 http://blog.al.com/breaking/2010/04/spacexs_elon_musk_sen_richard.html last online access March 13, 2013

S.3661; 2013; "Amendment to the Space Exploration Sustainability Act (H.R.6586.EAS)", *Congressional Record*, The Library of Congress, Washington DC, December 5 http://www.gpo.gov/fdsys/pkg/BILLS-112s3661is/pdf/BILLS-112s3661is.pdf last online access March 13, 2013

Sieff, Martin; 2012; "Shenzhou 9 keeps China's manned space program on course ", *Asia Pacific Defense Forum*, Camp H.M. Smith, Hawaii, July 12 http://apdforum.com/en_GB/article/rmiap/articles/online/features/2012/07/12/china-space-woman last online access March 13, 2013

Simberg, Rand; 2012; "Elon Musk on SpaceX's Reusable Rocket Plans", *Popular Mechanics*, New York, February 7, http://www.popularmechanics.com/science/space/rockets/elon-musk-on-spacexs-reusable-rocket-plans-6653023?click=pm_latest last online access March 13, 2013

Singer, Neil; 2007; "Sandia supercomputers offer new explanation of Tunguska disaster: Smaller asteroids may pose greater danger than previously believed", Sandia National Laboratories, Albuquerque, New Mexico, December 17, https://share.sandia.gov/news/resources/releases/2007/asteroid.html last online access March 13, 2013

Smith a, Stephen C.; 2012; "Posey's Power Grab", *Space KSC*, September 21 http://spaceksc.blogspot.com/2012/09/poseys-power-grab.html last online access March 13, 2013

Smith b, Stephen C.; 2012; "Posey Repeats False China Claims", *Space KSC*, July 23 http://spaceksc.blogspot.com/2012/07/posey-repeats-false-china-claims.html last online access March 13, 2013

Space Foundation; 2012; *Pioneering: Sustaining U.S. Leadership in Space*, Colorado Springs, Colorado http://www.spacefoundation.org/sites/default/files/downloads/PIONEERING.pdf last online access March 13, 2013

SpaceX a; 2012; "Falcon Heavy Overview", *SpaceX.com*, Space Exploration Technologies, Hawthorne, California http://www.spacex.com/falcon_heavy.php last online access March 13, 2013

SpaceX b; 2012; "NATIONAL PRESS CLUB LUNCHEON WITH ELON MUSK", *SpaceX.com*, Space Exploration Technologies, Hawthorne, California http://www.spacex.com/npc-luncheon-elon-musk.php last online access March 13, 2013

SpaceX c; 2012; "U.S. Air Force Evolved Expendable Launch Vehicle", *SpaceX.com*, Space Exploration Technologies, Hawthorne, California http://www.spacex.com/EELVBenefits.pdf

SpaceX d; 2008; "Falcon Launch Vehicle Payload User's Guide: Rev. 7", *SpaceX.com*, Space Exploration Technologies, Hawthorne, California page 13 http://www.spacex.com/Falcon1UsersGuide.pdf last online access March 13, 2013

SpaceX f; 2013; "Launch Manifest", Space Exploration Technologies, Hawthorne, California http://www.spacex.com/launch_manifest.php last online access March 28, 2013

StratoLaunch; 2012; "StratoLaunch Concept", *StratoLaunch Systems*, Huntsville, Alabama https://www.facebook.com/video/video.php?v=202596223158748 last online access March 13, 2013

Strickland a, John K. Jr.; 2011; "The SpaceX Falcon Heavy Booster: Why is it important?", *National Space Society*, Washington, DC , September http://www.nss.org/articles/falconheavy.html last online access March 13, 2013

Strickland b, John K. Jr.; 2011; "The SLS: too expensive for exploration?" *The Space Review*, November 28 http://www.thespacereview.com/article/1979/1 last online access March 13, 2013

Thomas, Mike; 2010; "More cash for NASA? That's one giant misstep", *The Orlando Sentinel*, Orlando, Florida, June 13 http://articles.orlandosentinel.com/2010-06-13/news/os-mike-thomas-elon-musk-061310-20100613_1_spacex-falcon-nasa last online access March 13, 2013

Tran, Huy K, Christine Johnson, Ming-Ta Hsu, H.C. Chem, Marnell Smith and Angie Chen-Johson; 1997; "Qualification of the forebody heatshield of the Stardust's Sample Return Capsule," AIAA, Thermophysics Conference, 32nd, Atlanta, GA; June 23-25 http://arc.aiaa.org/doi/abs/10.2514/6.1997-2482 last online access March 13, 2013

Tumlinson, Rick; 2011; "The Senate Launch System - Destiny, Decision, and Disaster", *The Huffington Post*, Washington, DC, September 15 http://www.huffingtonpost.com/rick-tumlinson/the-senate-launch-system-_b_963484.html last online access March 13, 2013

Walker, Robert and Charles Miller; 2013; "Commercial Space Exploration Needs an Obama Relaunch", *The Wall Street Journal*, New York, January 27 http://online.wsj.com/article/SB10001424127887324081704578233974117303116.html?mod=googlenews_wsj last online access March 13, 2013

Wilhite a, Alan; Douglas Stanley; Dale Arney; Chris Jones; 2010; *Near Term Space Exploration with Commercial Launch Vehicles Plus Propellant Depots*, Georgia Institute of Technology, Atlanta, Georgia, September 2 http://images.spaceref.com/news/2011/F9Prop.Depot.pdf last online access March 13, 2013

Wilhite b, Alan; Dale Arney; Christopher Jones; Patrick Chai; 2012; *Evolved Human Space Exploration Architecture Using Commercial Launch/Propellant Depots*, International Astronautical Federation, Paris, France IAC-12,D3,2,3,x15379 http://www.newspacewatch.com/docs/IAC-12.D3.2.3.x15379-NASAStudy.pdf last online access March 13, 2013

Wilhite c, Alan; 2013; *A Sustainable Evolved Human Space Exploration Architecture Using Commercial Launch and Propellant Depots*, Georgia Institute of Technology/National Institute of Aerospace, Atlanta, Georgia http://spirit.as.utexas.edu/~fiso/telecon/Wilhite_2-13-13/Wilhite_2-13-13.pdf last online access March 13, 2013

Williams, David and Tom Schatz; 2010; *NASA's Constellation Program: To Fly or Not To Fly*, Citizens Against Government Waste, Washington, DC, issue brief #02/2010, page 9

Wilson, Peter A.; 2013; "Kill The Space Launch System To Save Human Spaceflight", *Aviation Week*, April 1 https://www.aviationweek.com/awin/ArticlesStory.aspx?id=/article-xml/AW_04_01_2013_p66-563151.xml (behind paid firewall, subscription required)

Wolf, Frank; 2011; "WOLF STATEMENT AT U.S. - CHINA COMMISSION HEARING ON MILITARY AND CIVIL SPACE PROGRAMS IN CHINA" May 11 http://wolf.house.gov/index.cfm?sectionid=34&sectiontree=6,34&itemid=1724 last online access March 13, 2013

Zegler, Frank; Bernard F. Kutter; Jon Barr; 2009; *A Commercially Based Lunar Architecture*; United Launch Alliance, Denver, CO

http://ulalaunch.com/site/docs/publications/AffordableEx
plorationArchitecture2009.pdf last online access March 13,
2013

Zhang, Xiang; 2011; "China planning powerful carrier rocket
for manned moon landing", Xinhua News, March 3
http://news.xinhuanet.com/english2010/china/2011-
03/03/c_13759948.htm

Acknowledgements

During the first draft of the manuscript, the readability of this book was greatly enhanced by my wife, Julie Boozer. Her unwavering encouragement during this entire project was of paramount importance as well.

Clark Lindsey, the editor of the spaceflight industry publication *NewSpaceWatch.com*, was very gracious in his willingness to double check the information contained in the book. I was thrilled when he volunteered to do that for me because Clark is one of the most generally knowledgeable people there is as far as all things spaceflight-related. It amazed me that such a busy man and highly regarded space industry journalist would spend as much of his valuable time as he did to help me. Of course, many of his suggestions for improvement were incorporated in the final version of the book. There is no doubt the book is much better due to his input.

Leslie Ann Keller of the Astronomy Club of Asheville did me the favor of giving me the perspective of a nontechnical reader who is genuinely interested in the subject. Her feedback was truly invaluable.

As I mentioned in the Prologue, most of the ideas contained in this book were not my own. Any really great ideas came from the ones who significantly influenced me. Though I have never spoken to him in person, Buzz Aldrin has been an enormous inspiration to me as a person because he has come up with so many innovative ideas and was for years the *only one* of the Apollo astronauts who actively promoted the idea of using commercial launchers for human flight. During that time he took flak from some of his fellow astronauts for that stand. Kudos to Buzz for standing up for his principles all these years. I regret that his new book, *Mission to Mars: My Vision for Space Exploration* was not released in time for me to read it before I published this book. I am sure there must be a number of interesting things in it that I could have pointed out.

The aforementioned Clark Lindsey has had a significant effect on the evolution of my thoughts regarding the direction American spaceflight should take. The pioneering work of Rick Tumlinson aggressively pushed the concept of commercial spaceflight, leading to its prominent place in the limelight today and his influence cannot be overstated. Last but not least, my exposure to the thoughts of such minds as Jim Muncy, Jeff Foust, Jeff

Greason, Henry Vanderbilt, Gary Hudson, Keith Cowing, Doug Messier, Rand Simberg, Charles Lurio and many others cannot be discounted.

To the best of my ability, I went to great pains to insure that the information contained herein was accurate. Any mistakes found in this book should be totally attributed to me and did not come from any of the kind people who gave me their assistance.

Made in the USA
Lexington, KY
30 January 2014